FREE Test Taking Tips DVD Offer

To help us better serve you, we have developed a Test Taking Tips DVD that we would like to give you for FREE. **This DVD covers world-class test taking tips that you can use to be even more successful when you are taking your test.**

All that we ask is that you email us your feedback about your study guide. Please let us know what you thought about it – whether that is good, bad or indifferent.

To get your **FREE Test Taking Tips DVD**, email freedvd@studyguideteam.com with "FREE DVD" in the subject line and the following information in the body of the email:

> a. The title of your study guide.

> b. Your product rating on a scale of 1-5, with 5 being the highest rating.

> c. Your feedback about the study guide. What did you think of it?

> d. Your full name and shipping address to send your free DVD.

If you have any questions or concerns, please don't hesitate to contact us at freedvd@studyguideteam.com.

Thanks again!

Police Test Study Guide 2020 & 2021

Police Officer Exam Preparation Book & Practice Test Questions

Test Prep Books

Interested in buying more than 10 copies of our product? Contact us about bulk discounts:
bulkorders@studyguideteam.com

ISBN 13: 9781628457117
ISBN 10: 1628457112

Table of Contents

Quick Overview

As you draw closer to taking your exam, effective preparation becomes more and more important. Thankfully, you have this study guide to help you get ready. Use this guide to help keep your studying on track and refer to it often.

This study guide contains several key sections that will help you be successful on your exam. The guide contains tips for what you should do the night before and the day of the test. Also included are test-taking tips. Knowing the right information is not always enough. Many well-prepared test takers struggle with exams. These tips will help equip you to accurately read, assess, and answer test questions.

A large part of the guide is devoted to showing you what content to expect on the exam and to helping you better understand that content. In this guide are practice test questions so that you can see how well you have grasped the content. Then, answer explanations are provided so that you can understand why you missed certain questions.

Don't try to cram the night before you take your exam. This is not a wise strategy for a few reasons. First, your retention of the information will be low. Your time would be better used by reviewing information you already know rather than trying to learn a lot of new information. Second, you will likely become stressed as you try to gain a large amount of knowledge in a short amount of time. Third, you will be depriving yourself of sleep. So be sure to go to bed at a reasonable time the night before. Being well-rested helps you focus and remain calm.

Be sure to eat a substantial breakfast the morning of the exam. If you are taking the exam in the afternoon, be sure to have a good lunch as well. Being hungry is distracting and can make it difficult to focus. You have hopefully spent lots of time preparing for the exam. Don't let an empty stomach get in the way of success!

When travelling to the testing center, leave earlier than needed. That way, you have a buffer in case you experience any delays. This will help you remain calm and will keep you from missing your appointment time at the testing center.

Be sure to pace yourself during the exam. Don't try to rush through the exam. There is no need to risk performing poorly on the exam just so you can leave the testing center early. Allow yourself to use all of the allotted time if needed.

Remain positive while taking the exam even if you feel like you are performing poorly. Thinking about the content you should have mastered will not help you perform better on the exam.

Once the exam is complete, take some time to relax. Even if you feel that you need to take the exam again, you will be well served by some down time before you begin studying again. It's often easier to convince yourself to study if you know that it will come with a reward!

Test-Taking Strategies

1. Predicting the Answer

When you feel confident in your preparation for a multiple-choice test, try predicting the answer before reading the answer choices. This is especially useful on questions that test objective factual knowledge. By predicting the answer before reading the available choices, you eliminate the possibility that you will be distracted or led astray by an incorrect answer choice. You will feel more confident in your selection if you read the question, predict the answer, and then find your prediction among the answer choices. After using this strategy, be sure to still read all of the answer choices carefully and completely. If you feel unprepared, you should not attempt to predict the answers. This would be a waste of time and an opportunity for your mind to wander in the wrong direction.

2. Reading the Whole Question

Too often, test takers scan a multiple-choice question, recognize a few familiar words, and immediately jump to the answer choices. Test authors are aware of this common impatience, and they will sometimes prey upon it. For instance, a test author might subtly turn the question into a negative, or he or she might redirect the focus of the question right at the end. The only way to avoid falling into these traps is to read the entirety of the question carefully before reading the answer choices.

3. Looking for Wrong Answers

Long and complicated multiple-choice questions can be intimidating. One way to simplify a difficult multiple-choice question is to eliminate all of the answer choices that are clearly wrong. In most sets of answers, there will be at least one selection that can be dismissed right away. If the test is administered on paper, the test taker could draw a line through it to indicate that it may be ignored; otherwise, the test taker will have to perform this operation mentally or on scratch paper. In either case, once the obviously incorrect answers have been eliminated, the remaining choices may be considered. Sometimes identifying the clearly wrong answers will give the test taker some information about the correct answer. For instance, if one of the remaining answer choices is a direct opposite of one of the eliminated answer choices, it may well be the correct answer. The opposite of obviously wrong is obviously right! Of course, this is not always the case. Some answers are obviously incorrect simply because they are irrelevant to the question being asked. Still, identifying and eliminating some incorrect answer choices is a good way to simplify a multiple-choice question.

4. Don't Overanalyze

Anxious test takers often overanalyze questions. When you are nervous, your brain will often run wild, causing you to make associations and discover clues that don't actually exist. If you feel that this may be a problem for you, do whatever you can to slow down during the test. Try taking a deep breath or counting to ten. As you read and consider the question, restrict yourself to the particular words used by the author. Avoid thought tangents about what the author *really* meant, or what he or she was *trying* to say. The only things that matter on a multiple-choice test are the words that are actually in the question. You must avoid reading too much into a multiple-choice question, or supposing that the writer meant something other than what he or she wrote.

5. No Need for Panic

It is wise to learn as many strategies as possible before taking a multiple-choice test, but it is likely that you will come across a few questions for which you simply don't know the answer. In this situation, avoid panicking. Because most multiple-choice tests include dozens of questions, the relative value of a single wrong answer is small. As much as possible, you should compartmentalize each question on a multiple-choice test. In other words, you should not allow your feelings about one question to affect your success on the others. When you find a question that you either don't understand or don't know how to answer, just take a deep breath and do your best. Read the entire question slowly and carefully. Try rephrasing the question a couple of different ways. Then, read all of the answer choices carefully. After eliminating obviously wrong answers, make a selection and move on to the next question.

6. Confusing Answer Choices

When working on a difficult multiple-choice question, there may be a tendency to focus on the answer choices that are the easiest to understand. Many people, whether consciously or not, gravitate to the answer choices that require the least concentration, knowledge, and memory. This is a mistake. When you come across an answer choice that is confusing, you should give it extra attention. A question might be confusing because you do not know the subject matter to which it refers. If this is the case, don't eliminate the answer before you have affirmatively settled on another. When you come across an answer choice of this type, set it aside as you look at the remaining choices. If you can confidently assert that one of the other choices is correct, you can leave the confusing answer aside. Otherwise, you will need to take a moment to try to better understand the confusing answer choice. Rephrasing is one way to tease out the sense of a confusing answer choice.

7. Your First Instinct

Many people struggle with multiple-choice tests because they overthink the questions. If you have studied sufficiently for the test, you should be prepared to trust your first instinct once you have carefully and completely read the question and all of the answer choices. There is a great deal of research suggesting that the mind can come to the correct conclusion very quickly once it has obtained all of the relevant information. At times, it may seem to you as if your intuition is working faster even than your reasoning mind. This may in fact be true. The knowledge you obtain while studying may be retrieved from your subconscious before you have a chance to work out the associations that support it. Verify your instinct by working out the reasons that it should be trusted.

8. Key Words

Many test takers struggle with multiple-choice questions because they have poor reading comprehension skills. Quickly reading and understanding a multiple-choice question requires a mixture of skill and experience. To help with this, try jotting down a few key words and phrases on a piece of scrap paper. Doing this concentrates the process of reading and forces the mind to weigh the relative importance of the question's parts. In selecting words and phrases to write down, the test taker thinks about the question more deeply and carefully. This is especially true for multiple-choice questions that are preceded by a long prompt.

9. Subtle Negatives

One of the oldest tricks in the multiple-choice test writer's book is to subtly reverse the meaning of a question with a word like *not* or *except*. If you are not paying attention to each word in the question, you can easily be led astray by this trick. For instance, a common question format is, "Which of the following is…?" Obviously, if the question instead is, "Which of the following is not…?," then the answer will be quite different. Even worse, the test makers are aware of the potential for this mistake and will include one answer choice that would be correct if the question were not negated or reversed. A test taker who misses the reversal will find what he or she believes to be a correct answer and will be so confident that he or she will fail to reread the question and discover the original error. The only way to avoid this is to practice a wide variety of multiple-choice questions and to pay close attention to each and every word.

10. Reading Every Answer Choice

It may seem obvious, but you should always read every one of the answer choices! Too many test takers fall into the habit of scanning the question and assuming that they understand the question because they recognize a few key words. From there, they pick the first answer choice that answers the question they believe they have read. Test takers who read all of the answer choices might discover that one of the latter answer choices is actually *more* correct. Moreover, reading all of the answer choices can remind you of facts related to the question that can help you arrive at the correct answer. Sometimes, a misstatement or incorrect detail in one of the latter answer choices will trigger your memory of the subject and will enable you to find the right answer. Failing to read all of the answer choices is like not reading all of the items on a restaurant menu: you might miss out on the perfect choice.

11. Spot the Hedges

One of the keys to success on multiple-choice tests is paying close attention to every word. This is never truer than with words like almost, most, some, and sometimes. These words are called "hedges" because they indicate that a statement is not totally true or not true in every place and time. An absolute statement will contain no hedges, but in many subjects, the answers are not always straightforward or absolute. There are always exceptions to the rules in these subjects. For this reason, you should favor those multiple-choice questions that contain hedging language. The presence of qualifying words indicates that the author is taking special care with his or her words, which is certainly important when composing the right answer. After all, there are many ways to be wrong, but there is only one way to be right! For this reason, it is wise to avoid answers that are absolute when taking a multiple-choice test. An absolute answer is one that says things are either all one way or all another. They often include words like *every*, *always*, *best*, and *never*. If you are taking a multiple-choice test in a subject that doesn't lend itself to absolute answers, be on your guard if you see any of these words.

12. Long Answers

In many subject areas, the answers are not simple. As already mentioned, the right answer often requires hedges. Another common feature of the answers to a complex or subjective question are qualifying clauses, which are groups of words that subtly modify the meaning of the sentence. If the question or answer choice describes a rule to which there are exceptions or the subject matter is complicated, ambiguous, or confusing, the correct answer will require many words in order to be expressed clearly and accurately. In essence, you should not be deterred by answer choices that seem excessively long. Oftentimes, the author of the text will not be able to write the correct answer without

offering some qualifications and modifications. Your job is to read the answer choices thoroughly and completely and to select the one that most accurately and precisely answers the question.

13. Restating to Understand

Sometimes, a question on a multiple-choice test is difficult not because of what it asks but because of how it is written. If this is the case, restate the question or answer choice in different words. This process serves a couple of important purposes. First, it forces you to concentrate on the core of the question. In order to rephrase the question accurately, you have to understand it well. Rephrasing the question will concentrate your mind on the key words and ideas. Second, it will present the information to your mind in a fresh way. This process may trigger your memory and render some useful scrap of information picked up while studying.

14. True Statements

Sometimes an answer choice will be true in itself, but it does not answer the question. This is one of the main reasons why it is essential to read the question carefully and completely before proceeding to the answer choices. Too often, test takers skip ahead to the answer choices and look for true statements. Having found one of these, they are content to select it without reference to the question above. Obviously, this provides an easy way for test makers to play tricks. The savvy test taker will always read the entire question before turning to the answer choices. Then, having settled on a correct answer choice, he or she will refer to the original question and ensure that the selected answer is relevant. The mistake of choosing a correct-but-irrelevant answer choice is especially common on questions related to specific pieces of objective knowledge. A prepared test taker will have a wealth of factual knowledge at his or her disposal, and should not be careless in its application.

15. No Patterns

One of the more dangerous ideas that circulates about multiple-choice tests is that the correct answers tend to fall into patterns. These erroneous ideas range from a belief that B and C are the most common right answers, to the idea that an unprepared test-taker should answer "A-B-A-C-A-D-A-B-A." It cannot be emphasized enough that pattern-seeking of this type is exactly the WRONG way to approach a multiple-choice test. To begin with, it is highly unlikely that the test maker will plot the correct answers according to some predetermined pattern. The questions are scrambled and delivered in a random order. Furthermore, even if the test maker was following a pattern in the assignation of correct answers, there is no reason why the test taker would know which pattern he or she was using. Any attempt to discern a pattern in the answer choices is a waste of time and a distraction from the real work of taking the test. A test taker would be much better served by extra preparation before the test than by reliance on a pattern in the answers.

FREE DVD OFFER

Don't forget that doing well on your exam includes both understanding the test content and understanding how to use what you know to do well on the test. We offer a completely FREE Test Taking Tips DVD that covers world class test taking tips that you can use to be even more successful when you are taking your test.

All that we ask is that you email us your feedback about your study guide. To get your **FREE Test Taking Tips DVD**, email freedvd@studyguideteam.com with "FREE DVD" in the subject line and the following information in the body of the email:

- The title of your study guide.
- Your product rating on a scale of 1-5, with 5 being the highest rating.
- Your feedback about the study guide. What did you think of it?
- Your full name and shipping address to send your free DVD.

Introduction to the Police Officer Exam

Function of the Test

The Police Officer Exam was created to ensure the most capable individuals become officers and to give a general idea of what working as a police officer will entail. The test examines the credentials of an individual who wishes to become an officer and also their ability to make logical, informed decisions when interpreting the law. The most qualified candidate will be the one who is able to analyze each situation presented to them and develop a clear train of thought that will lead to the best possible action. The exam not only tests the individual on the law but on how to obtain and interpret data, make informed decisions, and provide clear, accurate reports of situations. The exam will also test the physical and mental aptitudes of its candidates to ensure they are fit to perform the duties required as an officer of the law. Those who successfully complete the exam will have a clearer understanding of the law in relation to real-life events, including what their duties will be when working on the job, and what skill they will need in the field to keep their communities and fellow officers safe.

Test Administration

The written test will be administered to those who, through their application and preliminary interview, prove to be the best-qualified candidates for the job. Depending on the district, the written test will most likely be taken in a class-like environment hosted by the department, who will provide the location specifications to the test taker when arranged. The test will be taken in a group setting but with individual designated areas for each test taker to ensure there is no sharing or copying of answers. Test-taking materials will be provided to each applicant upon arrival. Depending on the district, the test may be given as a physical copy or on a secure computer with questions preprogrammed. The individual should, if possible, have a clear schedule on the day of the test so they have the most time available for completion. A test proctor will be at the location to answer any questions or concerns an individual may have when taking the test. Brief breaks may also be offered, but the written test should be completed within the same day. Water or light refreshments may also be brought or provided, but applicants should check first with their test administrator.

Test Format

Although the details of a police exam may differ slightly depending on location, there are a few main components of every exam. The written exam will consist of interpreting and analyzing information to test basic skills needed to reach logical conclusions about how to act given a specific situation. However, more generally, the exam will test the individual's reading comprehension, math, grammar, analytical skills, and ability to make logical deductions. Someone who is successful on the test will have a basic understanding of how to interpret and use written data and descriptions. Questions relating to reading and interpreting visual data will also be included. The officer needs to have a general awareness of their surroundings and the ways people travel and interact with each other. The police exam also tests the physical and mental aptitudes of the test taker to determine if they are healthy enough to perform their required duties. The polygraph and personal interview portions of the test will examine the individual's ability to communicate clearly and honestly. Altogether, the different components of the test are combined to determine the most sound, capable individuals for police work to ensure the safety of the community.

Scoring

The police exam is scored with a percentage based on correct answers given, especially for the written portion of the exam. The questions have predetermined right and wrong answers, and most will be in the multiple-choice style. The test can usually run from 100 to 200 questions, with a passing score given to those who answer at least 70 percent or more correct (which could be higher depending on the jurisdiction). Each test will be scored individually by a professional who has been designated by the department. Scores will then be given in private to each test taker upon completion of grading. However, higher test scores do not always correlate with the most successful officers because on-the-job training will be the next determining factor of success as an officer. The test itself is more of a way to examine whether or not an individual possesses all the basic knowledge needed to perform their job. Those with passing scores will be the ones who have been judged to be physically and mentally capable of handling the mental and physical demands of police work and are considered stable enough to not present a risk to the safety of others.

Police Careers

Hierarchy of Duties

The police force is organized as a hierarchy of individuals with different roles. This hierarchy defines the police power and organizational structure in a country. An officer should be familiar with their role in the unit and the imposed limits on their position. An officer should also be aware of their supervisors and the role they play in the hierarchy of duties. Every officer will need to know and report to at least one superior in their unit for clear instructions relating to their role. In the United States, although some of the exact names of titles may be different, the general hierarchy of police officer ranks is as follows: The officer reports to the detective; the detective to the sergeant; the sergeant to the police captain; the police captain to the major or deputy inspector; the major to the inspector; the inspector to the deputy chief; and the deputy chief to the chief of police. Each role has its own protocol for reporting to a superior and managing those beneath them. In the police force, is important to know what is expected of each member in order to clearly define the chain of command and the correct actions that can be taken as determined by the hierarchy of duties.

Choosing a Location

Every location will have slightly different day-to-day operations, but each will adhere to state and federal protocols that have been put in place by legislature. When entering the police force, an officer may have the chance to determine what location they would like to work in. When choosing a location, it is first important to determine what area will be in proximity to where they live. Most officers will want a location that is closer to home to avoid unnecessary travel time to and from work. Also important to consider when choosing a location to work is identifying which areas are in the most need of help. An officer will be able to make the most impact in an underserved area where they will receive the most work and have the best opportunity to improve the community.

Preparing Yourself

An officer needs to be prepared for their future career so they can have the best chance of success. The amount of information that needs to be learned may seem daunting. However, with good study habits and an understanding of what will be expected, the chance of succeeding will be greater. The most successful officers will be the ones who have clear ideas of what is expected of them and what they can do to be the best they can within their abilities. An officer becomes most familiar with their duties by working and training on the job, but the test will be the factor that determines if they have a basic knowledge and understanding of what their general responsibilities will be, including how to reason effectively when presented with a case.

The best preparation for the police exam and work as an officer is to be familiar with the law. The law is the deciding factor behind most officer actions, and those who are familiar with the legal system in their country work will have a better chance at interpreting scenarios in relation to the law. Other ways to prepare is to research how others have passed the test and what strategies they used to determine correct answers. It is a good idea to look up as many practice situations as possible and become familiar with where and how officers collect and use data. Also, it is important to remember to stay calm and know that regardless of the outcome, there will always be more opportunities for success in the future.

Application Process

Finding Job Opportunities

It is important to be aware of all the resources available when looking for the right **job opportunity** in the police force. The individual should also have a general idea of what their skill set is and how their past work or school experience will be useful in a police career. Once they have an understanding of their strengths and weaknesses, they are better at marketing themselves to potential employers. The individual should next find out where they can discover the positions that best fit them. The internet will be a very helpful tool when searching for available jobs. The job seeker should also have a clear idea of where they are willing to work in order to narrow their search to positions in their area. Once an area and a type of job have been determined, the individual can conduct specific searches to learn about the best opportunities.

Minimum Requirements

There are certain **minimum requirements** to be eligible for work in the police force. The first requirement is a high school diploma or GED, as well as completing the police exam. For other positions, a college degree may also be required. The individual must also be a resident living in the United States to work as a U.S. police officer. Another important requirement is having a clean record with no previous felony or misdemeanor charges. A background check is performed on all officers before employment to ensure each has a history of law compliance. Anyone with previous charges or who is restricted from driving an automobile will not be admitted. An applicant will also need to pass the physical and psychological portions of the police exam to be deemed fit to serve in the police force.

Filling Out the Application

The first step to becoming a police officer is **filling out an application**. Most applications will be completed and filled out online. It is important for the applicant to provide accurate information because each candidate will be background checked to ensure they have not used misleading data in order to better their chances at obtaining a position. Individuals should follow the layout of the application, which will clearly label where to input each type of information. They should also double-check the application before submission to catch any errors that may have been made. Information filled out on the application should be clear, with specific dates and names where required. Due to the large number of applications received, the applicant should also be prepared to wait for all the information to be processed. If they are selected based on their application, they will be contacted with information on how to proceed with the next steps of the hiring process.

Physical Test/Preliminary Medical Review

In addition to the written exam, potential officers will also need to complete a **physical test/preliminary medical review** to make sure they are physically fit enough to handle the active responsibilities of their position. The physical exam consists of activities that test stamina, speed, and strength. Although some departments may differ in the exact tests performed, in general a potential officer will need to complete a set number of push-ups and sit-ups in addition to testing their ability to run long distances and sprint short distances. A person is considered to have passed the physical test if they can fully complete all the required activities without concern or medical issues. A medical review will also assess the individual's health, determining if they are able to perform the responsibilities required of their position without any

debilitating health risks. The best way for applicants to prepare for the physical test and medical review is to remain active and regularly see a physician to maintain good health and exercise habits. Even if someone is not the most physically fit, they can still pass this portion of the exam if they have already trained toward an active lifestyle and are used to physical activity.

The Psychological Exam

The **psychological portion of the police exam** is used to test the general intelligence and mental health of the potential officer. This exam tests the individual's suitability for the job. Those who pass the psychological exam are deemed to be mentally capable of managing the day-to-day responsibilities of being an officer, which can sometimes involve highly emotional and dangerous situations. An officer needs to be stable enough to stay calm under these extreme mental states. They also need to be able to keep a level of professionalism and mental clarity at all times when representing themselves as officers.

The psychological exam will measure the individual's judgment, reasoning skills, and personality traits. The applicant should be prepared to answer situational questions related to the job as well as more personal questions related to their mental wellbeing. Personality traits deemed most important to success in the police force, such as honesty, courage, and sound judgment, will be measured for the individual in relation to those who are already working as officers. Those with high temperaments or an inability to control impulses will not be considered because of their greater chance of impaired judgment when determining actions to take. An individual who can speak calmly and comprehensively about events will have the best chance of passing the psychological test. It is also important for applicants to not be too flustered or anxious during the test so they present themselves as being able to manage high-stress situations that often occur in the line of police work.

The Polygraph Test

The **polygraph test** is used to determine the truthfulness of the candidate and to verify that the individual has not violated any of the determined conditions that need to be met to become an officer. Questions will be direct and relate to specific crimes or instances that the individual will need to respond to with either a yes or no answer. Questions will be asked about past drug use or possible crimes committed. General questions about the individual will also be asked to determine their truthfulness.

The most important thing for applicants to remember when taking the polygraph test is to remain honest. A passing test means the individual did not lie. Polygraphs do not necessarily test the information given but identify changes in behavior, such as increased heart rate, when a lie is being told. This is why it is also important for potential officers to remain as calm as possible when taking the polygraph test so the machine does not detect that their body is lying when they are in fact telling the truth. It may seem intimidating, but the right candidate will be able to overcome any anxieties about the test if they remain calm and truthful. Those with nothing to hide do the best on this portion of the test because they know that what they say is the truth, and their body reflects this.

The Interview

The first way to learn about an individual and determine if they are the right fit to become an officer is the **interview process**. This is the time when the most general questions about a person's past and work history are addressed. It is the chance for the candidate to detail their skills and professional history. It is also a way to show they can have formal conversations in a professional manner that can be easily understood by others. The personality of the individual can also be assessed according to how they interact and carry on a conversation with the interviewer.

A standard interview will proceed first with introductions between the interviewer and the interviewee. Then, the candidate may be asked why they want to join the police force or what makes them fit for the job. It can be helpful for an applicant to prepare an answer to these questions before the interview in order to have a clear idea of how to best present themselves. The interviewee will also get a chance to ask about what their role may be if they obtain the position and how the individual district they are applying for differs from others. The interview should not be construed as a series of questions but as a general dialogue between individuals to assess how they communicate with others. Often, speaking in an agreeable, professional manner will be more helpful in the interview process than the actual answers given because the interview is more of a chance for others to get a feel for how a potential officer communicates as a unique individual, and how they can present themselves as a valuable member of the team.

Spelling

Police officers are expected to express themselves with authority. Choosing the best words for each situation is only part of this task. Being able to spell those words correctly is also crucial. For this reason, their aptitude for spelling is measured on the exam. Consider, too, that accurate spelling helps to convey competence and professionalism.

The spelling test portion of the exam usually includes around fifteen multiple-choice items, each featuring a sentence with one word omitted. The answer choices will present four different spellings of the same word, only one of which is correct. Test takers will be asked to identify the correct spelling.

Importance of Prefixes and Suffixes

The most common spelling mistakes are made when a **root word** (or a basic, core word) is modified by adding a prefix or a suffix to it. A **prefix** is a group of letters added to the beginning of a word, and a **suffix** is a group of letters added to the end of a word.

The prefixes usually change the meaning of the word. They might be negative or positive and signal time, location, or number. Note the spelling of the root word does not change when adding a prefix.

Common Prefixes		
Prefix	Meaning	Example
dis-	not, opposite	disagree, disproportionate
en-, em-	to make, to cause	encode, embrace
in-, im-	in, into	induct
ir-, il-, im-	not, opposite	impossible, irresponsible
mis-	bad, wrongly	misfire, mistake
mono-	alone, one	monologue
non-	not, opposite	nonsense
over-	more than, too much	overlook
pre-	before	precede
post-	after	postmortem
re-	again, back	review
un-	not, opposite	unacceptable

A suffix can change the base word in two ways:

- Change numerical agreement: turns a singular word into a plural word (a singular witness becomes plural witnesses)

- Change grammatical function: turns one part of speech into another (noun to verb, verb to adverb), such as moderation, moderating, or moderately

Common Suffixes		
Suffix	Meaning/Use	Example
-able, -ible	able to	unbearable, plausible
-ance	state of being	significance
-al, -ial	relating to	lethal, testimonial, criminal
-ceed, -sede, -cede	go, go forward, withdraw, yield	exceed, recede, supersede
-ed	changes root word to past tense or past participle	called, played
-en	makes root word a verb	heighten, liven
-er	more, action, a person who does an action	clearer, sever, believer
-ful	full of	hateful, beautiful
-ian, -ite	person who does the action, part of a group	politician, meteorite
-ice, -ize	cause, treat, become	service, popularize
-ing	action	writing, playing
-ion, -tion	action or condition	celebration, organization
-ism	forms nouns referring to beliefs or behavior	Buddhism, recidivism
-ity, -ty	state of being	adversity, cruelty
-ive, -tive	state or quality	defensive, conservative
-less	without	tactless, nameless
-ly	in such a manner	poorly, happily
-ment	action	endorsement, disagreement
-ness	makes root word a noun referring to a state of being	weakness, kindness
-or	a person who does an action	moderator, perpetrator
-s, -es	makes root word plural	weights, boxes
-sion	state of being	admission, immersion
-y	made up of	moody, greasy

Doubling-Up Consonants (or Not)

When adding some suffixes (usually, *-ing*, *-sion*) to a root word that ends in one vowel followed immediately by one consonant, *double that last consonant*.

Base Word	Vowel/consonant	Suffix	Spelling Change
wrap	a, p	-ing	wra*pp*ing
canvas	a,s		canva*ss*ing
admit	i, t	-sion	admi*ss*ion

This rule does not apply to multi-vowel words, such as *sleep*, *treat*, and *appear*. When attaching a suffix that begins with a vowel to a word with a multi-letter vowel followed by a consonant, *do not double the consonant*.

Base Word	Multi-vowel, consonant	Suffix	Spelling
sleep	ee, p	-ing	slee*p*ing
treat	ea, t	-ed	trea*t*ed
appear	ea, r	-ance	appea*r*ance

Do *not* double the consonant if the root word already ends in a double consonant or the letter *x* (examples—*add/adding, fox/foxes*).

Words Ending with *y* or *c*

If a root word ends in a single vowel *y*, the *y* should be changed to *i* when adding any suffix, unless that suffix begins with the letter *i*. If a root word ends in a two-letter vowel, such as *oy*, *ay*, or *ey*, the *y* is kept.

Root Word	Ending	Suffix	Spelling Change
baby	y	-ed	babied
stymy	y		stymied
crony	y	-ism	cronyism
say	y	-ing	saying
annoy	oy	-ance	annoyance
survey	ey	-ing	surveying

In cases where the root word is a verb (ending with the letter *c*) and the suffix begins with an *e, i,* or *y,* the letter *k* is added to the end of the word between the last letter and the suffix.

Root Word	Ending	Suffix	Spelling Change
panic	ic	-ing	panicking
		-y	panicky
traffic	ic	-ed	trafficked
		-er	trafficker

Words with *ie* or *ei*

There's an old saying "*I* before *E*, except after *C*." There's also a second part to it:

> *I* before *E*,
>
> Except after *C*,
>
> Or when sounded as *A*,
>
> As in *neighbor* and *weigh*.

Here are a few examples:

- *friend, wield, yield* (*i* before *e*)
- *receipt, deceive* (except after *c*)
- *weight, freight* (or when sounded as *a*)

Words Ending in *e*

Generally, the *e* at the end of English words is silent or not pronounced (e.g., *bake*).

- If the suffix being added to a root word begins with a consonant, keep the *e*.
- If the suffix begins with a vowel, the final silent *e* is dropped.

Root Word	Ending	Suffix	Spelling Change
waste remorse pause	silent *e*	-ful -s	wasteful remorseful pauses
reserve pause	silent *e*	-ation -ing	reservation pausing

Exceptions: When the root word ends in *ce* or *ge* and the suffix –*able* or –*ous* is being added, the silent final *e* is kept (e.g., *courageous, noticeable*).

Words Ending with -*ise* or -*ize*

Sometimes, it can be difficult to tell whether a word (usually a verb) should end in –*ise* or –*ize*. In American English, only a few words end with –*ise*. A few examples are *advertise, advise,* and *compromise*. Most words are more likely to end in –*ize*. A few examples are *accessorize, authorize, capitalize,* and *legalize*.

Words Ending with -*ceed, -sede,* or -*cede*

It can also be difficult to tell whether a word should end in –*ceed*, –*sede*, or –*cede*. In the English language, there are only three words that end with –*ceed*: *exceed, proceed,* and *succeed*. There is only one word that ends with –*sede*: *supersede*.

If a word other than *supersede* ends in a suffix that sounds like –*sede,* it should probably be –*cede*. For example: *concede, recede,* and *precede*.

Words Ending in *–able* or *–ible*

In the English language, more words end in *–able* than in *–ible:*

- e.g., probable, actionable, approachable, traceable
- e.g., accessible, admissible, plausible

Words Ending in *-ance* or *-ence*

The suffixes *-ance* and *-ence* are added to verbs to change them into nouns or adjectives that refer to a state of being. For example, when *-ance* is added to the verb *perform*, *performance* is formed, referring to the act of performing.

Suffix	When to use	Example
-ance, -ancy, -ant	<ul><li>When the root word ends in a *c* that sounds like *k*</li><li>When the root word ends in a hard *g*</li></ul>	<ul><li>significance</li><li>arrogance</li><li>vacancy</li><li>extravagant</li></ul>
-ence, -ency, -ent	<ul><li>When the root word ends in a *c* that sounds like *s*</li><li>When the root word ends in a *g* that sounds like *j*</li></ul>	<ul><li>adolescence</li><li>convergence</li><li>contingency</li><li>convergent</li></ul>

Words Ending in *-tion, -sion,* or *-cian*

The suffixes *–tion* and *–sion* are used when forming nouns that refer to the result of a verb. For example, the result of *to abbreviate something* is an *abbreviation*. Likewise, if a person has *compressed* something, then there is a *compression*.

The suffix *–cian* is used when referring to a person who practices something specific. For example, the person who practices *politics* is a *politician*.

Words Containing *-ai* or *-ia*

Unfortunately, there isn't an easy-to-remember rhyme for deciding whether a word containing the vowels *a* and *i* should be spelled *ai* or *ia.* In this case, it's helpful to rely on pronunciation to determine the correct spelling.

The combination of *ai* is one sound, as in the words capt*ai*n or f*ai*nt.

The combination of *ia*, on the other hand, is two separate sounds, as in the words guard*ia*n and d*ia*bolical.

It's helpful to say the word out loud to decide which combination of the two vowels is correct.

Rules for Plural Nouns

Nouns Ending in *-ch, -sh, -s, -x,* or *-z*

When modifying a noun that ends in *ch, sh, s, x,* or *z* to its plural form, add *es* instead of the singular *s.* For example, *trench* becomes *trenches, ash* becomes *ashes, business* becomes *businesses, jukebox* becomes *jukeboxes,* and *fox* becomes *foxes.*

This rule also applies to family names. For example, the Finch family becomes the *Finches,* and the Martinez family becomes the *Martinezes.*

Nouns Ending in *y* or *ay, ey, iy, oy,* or *uy*

When forming plurals with nouns ending in the consonant *y,* the *y* is replaced with *-ies.* For example, *spy* becomes *spies,* and *city* becomes *cities.*

If a noun ends with a vowel before a *y,* the *y* is kept, and an *s* is added. For example, *key* becomes *keys,* and *foray* becomes *forays.*

Nouns Ending in *f* or *fe*

When forming plurals with nouns ending in *f* or *fe,* the *f* is replaced with *v,* and *es* is added. For example, *half* becomes *halves,* and *knife* becomes *knives.*

Some exceptions are *roof/roofs* and *reef/reefs.*

Nouns Ending in *o*

When forming plurals with nouns ending in a consonant and *o,* the *o* is kept and an *es* is added. For example, *tomato* becomes *tomatoes.*

Musical terms are the exception to this rule. Words like *soprano* and *piano* are pluralized by adding *s* even though they end in a consonant and *o* (*sopranos, pianos*).

When forming plurals with nouns ending in a vowel and *o,* the *o* is kept, and *s* is added. For example, *ratio* becomes *ratios,* and *patio* becomes *patios.*

Exceptions to the Rules of Plurals

For some nouns, instead of changing or adding letters at the end of the word, changes to the vowels within the words are necessary. For example:

- *man* becomes *men*
- woman becomes women
- child becomes children

Some nouns, when pluralized, change entirely:

- tooth becomes teeth
- *foot* becomes *feet*
- *mouse* becomes *mice*

The opposite is also true; some nouns are the same in the plural as they are in the singular form. For example, *deer, species, fish,* and *sheep* are all plural nouns in singular form.

Practice Questions

Directions: In the following sentences, choose the correct spelling of the missing word.

1. The suspect fled the _____ on foot.
    a. seen
    b. scene
    c. sceen
    d. sene

2. The fugitive was _____ only a few blocks from his home.
    a. apprehanded
    b. aprended
    c. apprehended
    d. aprehended

3. The new officer has high hopes to one day be promoted all the way to _____.
    a. captain
    b. captin
    c. captian
    d. captan

4. It was his first day on the job and he didn't want to make any _____.
    a. mistaks
    b. misstakes
    c. mistakes
    d. mitsakes

5. This was his first time to get to _____ such a serious crime.
    a. invistagate
    b. investigate
    c. envestigate
    d. investagate

Answer Explanations

1. B

2. C

3. A

4. C

5. B

Enforcement Vocabulary

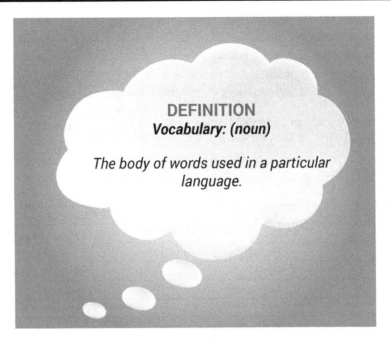

Vocabulary is simply the words a person uses and understands on a daily basis. Having a good vocabulary is important in both written and verbal communications. In law enforcement, officers may have to read court records, police reports, and other legal documents. Many of these materials may contain unfamiliar words, so it's important for officers to learn ways to uncover a word's meaning so they can use it correctly in their own writing.

To understand the challenges of using vocabulary correctly, imagine suddenly being thrust into a foreign country. Not knowing the right words to use when asking for basic necessities (e.g., food, a place to stay, a bathroom) would make everyday life extremely difficult. Asking for help from people who don't share the same vocabulary is hard, since language is what facilitates understanding between people. The more vocabulary words a person understands, the more precisely they can communicate their intentions. This section of the study guide focuses on understanding and deciphering vocabulary through basic grammar.

Prefixes and Suffixes

In the previous section, we went over the particular spelling of prefixes and suffixes, and how they changed the root word. In this section, we will look at the meaning of various prefixes and suffixes when added to a root word. As mentioned before, a prefix is a combination of letters found at the beginning of a word, while a suffix is a combination of letters found at the end. A **root word** is the word that comes after the prefix, before the suffix, or between them both. Sometimes a root word can stand on its own without either a prefix or a suffix. More simply put:

Prefix + Root Word = Word

Root Word + Suffix = Word

Prefix + Root Word + Suffix = Word

Root Word = Word

Knowing the definitions of common prefixes and suffixes can help when trying to determine the meaning of an unknown word. In addition, knowing prefixes can help in determining the number of things, the negative of something, or the time and space of an object. Understanding suffix definitions can help when trying to determine the meaning of an adjective, noun, or verb.

The following charts review some of the most common prefixes, what they mean, and how they're used to decipher a word's meaning.

Number and Quantity Prefixes

Prefix	Definition	Example
bi-	two	bicycle, bilateral
mono-	one, single	monopoly, monotone
poly-	many	polygamy, polygon
semi-	half, partly	semiannual, semicircle
uni-	one	unicycle, universal

Here's an example of a number prefix:

The countries signed a *bilateral* agreement; both had to abide by the contract.

Look at the word *bilateral*. If the root word (*lateral*) is unfamiliar, the prefix (*bi-*) can provide a vital clue to its meaning. The prefix *bi-* means *two*, which shows that the agreement involves two of something, most likely the two countries, since *both had to abide by the contract*. This is correct since *bilateral* actually means "involving two parties, usually countries."

Negative Prefixes

Prefix	Definition	Example
a-	without, lack of	amoral, atypical
in-	not, opposing	inability, inverted
non-	not	nonexistent, nonstop
un-	not, reverse	unable, unspoken

Here's an example of a negative prefix:

The patient's *inability* to speak made the doctor wonder what was wrong.

Look at the word *inability*. In the chart above, the prefix *in-* means *not* or *opposing*. By replacing the prefix with *not* and placing it in front of the root word of *ability* (*able*), the meaning of the word becomes clear: *not able*. Therefore, the patient was *not able* to speak.

Time and Space Prefixes

Prefix	Definition	Example
a-	in, on, of, up, to	aloof, associate
ab-	from, away, off	abstract, absent
ad-	to, towards	adept, adjacent
ante-	before, previous	antebellum, antenna
anti-	against, opposing	anticipate, antisocial
cata-	down, away, thoroughly	catacomb, catalogue
circum-	around	circumstance, circumvent
com-	with, together, very	combine, compel
contra-	against, opposing	contraband, contrast
de-	from	decrease, descend
dia-	through, across, apart	diagram, dialect
dis-	away, off, down, not	disregard, disrespect
epi-	upon	epidemic, epiphany
ex-	out	example, exit
hypo-	under, beneath	hypoallergenic, hypothermia
inter-	among, between	intermediate, international
intra-	within	intrapersonal, intravenous
ob-	against, opposing	obtain, obscure
per-	through	permanent, persist
peri-	around	periodontal, periphery
post-	after, following	postdate, postoperative
pre-	before, previous	precede, premeditate
pro-	forward, in place of	program, propel
retro-	back, backward	retroactive, retrofit
sub-	under, beneath	submarine, substantial
super-	above, extra	superior, supersede
trans-	across, beyond, over	transform, transmit
ultra-	beyond, excessively	ultraclean, ultralight

Here's an example of a space prefix:

> The teacher's motivational speech helped *propel* her students toward greater academic achievement.

Look at the word *propel*. The prefix *pro-* means *forward* or *in place of* which indicates something relevant to time and space. *Propel* means to drive or move in a direction (usually forward), so knowing the prefix *pro-* helps interpret that the students are moving forward *toward greater academic achievement.*

Miscellaneous Prefixes

Prefix	Definition	Example
belli-	war, warlike	bellied, belligerent
bene-	well, good	benediction, beneficial
equi-	equal	equidistant, equinox
for-	away, off, from	forbidden, forsaken
fore-	previous	forecast, forebode
homo-	same, equal	homogeneous, homonym
hyper-	excessive, over	hyperextend, hyperactive
in-	in, into	insignificant, invasive
magn-	large	magnetic, magnificent
mal-	bad, poorly, not	maladapted, malnourished
mis-	wrongly, mistaken	misplace, misguide
mor-	death	mortal, morgue
neo-	new	neoclassical, neonatal
omni-	all, everywhere	omnipotent, omnipresent
ortho-	right, straight	orthodontist, orthopedic
over-	above	overload, overstock,
pan-	all, entire	panacea, pander
para-	beside, beyond	paradigm, parameter
phil-	love, like	philanthropy, philosophic
prim-	first, early	primal, primer
re-	backward, again	reload, regress
sym-	with, together	symmetry, symbolize
vis-	to see	visual, visibility

Here's another prefix example:

The computer was *primitive*; it still had a floppy disk drive!

The word *primitive* has the prefix *prim-* which indicates being *first* or *early*. *Primitive* means the historical development of something. Therefore, the sentence infers that the computer is an older model because it no longer has a floppy disk drive.

The charts that follow review some of the most common suffixes and include examples of how they're used to determine the meaning of a word. Remember, suffixes are added to the *end* of a root word.

Adjective Suffixes

Suffix	Definition	Example
-able (-ible)	capable of being	teachable, accessible
-esque	in the style of, like	humoresque, statuesque
-ful	filled with, marked by	helpful, deceitful
-ic	having, containing	manic, elastic
-ish	suggesting, like	malnourish, tarnish
-less	lacking, without	worthless, fearless
-ous	marked by, given to	generous, previous

Here's an example of an adjective suffix:

The live model looked so *statuesque* in the window display; she didn't even move!

Look at the word *statuesque*. The suffix *-esque* means *in the style of* or *like*. If something is *statuesque*, it's *in the style of a statue* or *like a statue*. In this sentence, the model looks *like* a statue.

Noun Suffixes

Suffix	Definition	Example
-acy	state, condition	literacy, legacy
-ance	act, condition, fact	distance, importance
-ard	one that does	leotard, billiard
-ation	action, state, result	legislation, condemnation
-dom	state, rank, condition	freedom, kingdom
-er (-or)	office, action	commuter, spectator
-ess	feminine	caress, princess
-hood	state, condition	childhood, livelihood
-ion	action, result, state	communion, position
-ism	act, manner, doctrine	capitalism, patriotism
-ist	worker, follower	stylist, activist
-ity (-ty)	state, quality, condition	community, dirty
-ment	result, action	empowerment, segment
-ness	quality, state	fitness, rudeness
-ship	position	censorship, leadership
-sion (-tion)	state, result	tension, transition
-th	act, state, quality	twentieth, wealth
-tude	quality, state, result	attitude, latitude

Look at the following example of a noun suffix:

The *spectator* cheered when his favorite soccer team scored a goal.

Look at the word *spectator*. The suffix *-or* means *action*. In this sentence, the *action* is to *spectate* (watch something), thus a *spectator* is someone involved in watching something.

Verb Suffixes

Suffix	Definition	Example
-ate	having, showing	facilitate, integrate
-en	cause to be, become	frozen, written
-fy	make, cause to have	modify, rectify
-ize	cause to be, treat with	realize, sanitize

Here's an example of a verb suffix:

> The preschool had to *sanitize* the toys every Tuesday and Thursday.

In the word *sanitize*, the suffix *-ize* means *cause to be* or *treat with*. By adding the suffix *-ize* to the root word *sanitary*, the meaning of the word becomes active: *cause to be sanitary*.

Context Clues

It's common to encounter unfamiliar words in written communication. When faced with an unknown word, there are certain "tricks" that can be used to uncover its meaning. **Context clues** are words or phrases within a sentence or paragraph that provide hints about a word and its definition. For example, if an unfamiliar word is anchored to a noun with other attached words as clues, these can help decipher the word's meaning. Consider the following example:

> After the treatment, Grandma's natural rosy cheeks looked *wan* and ghostlike.

The unfamiliar word is *wan*. The first clue to its meaning is in the phrase *After the treatment,* which implies that something happened after a procedure (possibly medical). A second clue is the word *rosy,* which describes Grandma's natural cheek color that changed after the treatment. Finally, the word *ghostlike* infers that Grandma's cheeks now look white. By using the context clues in the sentence, the meaning of the word *wan* (which means *pale*) can be deciphered.

Below are some additional ways to use context clues to uncover the meaning of an unknown word.

Contrasts

Look for context clues that **contrast** the unknown word. When reading a sentence with an unfamiliar word, look for a contrasting or opposing word or idea. Here's an example:

> Since Mary didn't cite her research sources, she lost significant points for *plagiarizing* the content of her report.

In this sentence, *plagiarizing* is the unfamiliar word. Notice that when Mary *didn't cite her research sources,* it resulted in her losing points for *plagiarizing the content of her report*. These contrasting ideas infer that Mary did something wrong with the content. This makes sense because the definition of *plagiarizing* is "taking the work of someone else and passing it off as your own."

Contrasts often use words like *but, however, although,* or phrases like *on the other hand.* For example:

The *gargantuan* television won't fit in my car, but it will cover the entire wall in the den.

The unfamiliar word is *gargantuan.* Notice that the television is too big to fit in a car, <u>*but it will cover the entire wall in the den.*</u> This infers that the television is extremely large, which is correct, since the word *gargantuan* means "enormous."

Synonyms

Another method is to brainstorm possible synonyms for the unknown word. **Synonyms** are words with the same or similar meanings (e.g., *strong* and *sturdy*). To do this, substitute synonyms one at a time, reading the sentence after each to see if the meaning is clear. By replacing an unknown word with a known one, it may be possible to uncover its meaning. For example:

Gary's clothes were *saturated* after he fell into the swimming pool.

In this sentence, the word *saturated* is unknown. To brainstorm synonyms for *saturated,* think about what happens to Gary's clothes after falling into the swimming pool. They'd be *soaked* or *wet,* both of which turn out to be good synonyms to try since the actual meaning of *saturated* is "thoroughly soaked."

Antonyms

Sometimes sentences contain words or phrases that oppose each other. Opposite words are known as **antonyms** (e.g., *hot* and *cold*). For example:

Although Mark seemed *tranquil,* you could tell he was actually nervous as he paced up and down the hall.

The unknown word here is *tranquil.* The sentence says that Mark was in fact not *tranquil* but was instead *actually nervous.* The opposite of the word *nervous* is *calm,* which is the meaning of the word *tranquil.*

Explanations or Descriptions

Explanations or descriptions of other things in the sentence can also provide clues to an unfamiliar word. Take the following example:

Golden Retrievers, Great Danes, and Pugs are the top three *breeds* competing in the dog show.

If the word *breeds* is unknown, look at the sentence for an explanation or description that provides a clue. The subjects (*Golden Retrievers, Great Danes,* and *Pugs*) describe different types of dogs. This description helps uncover the meaning of the word *breeds* which is "a particular type or group of animals."

Inferences

Sometimes there are clues to an unknown word that infer or suggest its meaning. These **inferences** can be found either within the sentence where the word appears or in a sentence that precedes or follows it. Look at the following example:

The *wretched* old lady was kicked out of the restaurant. She was so mean and nasty to the waiter!

Here the word *wretched* is unknown. The first sentence states that the *old lady was kicked out of the restaurant*, but it doesn't say why. The sentence that follows tells us why: *She was so mean and nasty to the waiter!* This infers that the old lady was *kicked out* because she was *so mean and nasty* or, in other words, *wretched*.

When preparing for a vocabulary test, try reading challenging materials to learn new words. If a word on the test is unfamiliar, look for prefixes and suffixes to help uncover what the word means and eliminate incorrect answers. If two answers both seem right, determine if there are any differences between them and then select the word that best fits. Context clues in the sentence or paragraph can also help to uncover the meaning of an unknown word. By learning new vocabulary words, a person can expand their knowledge base and improve the quality and effectiveness of their written communications.

Practice Questions

Directions: Read each sentence carefully and select the answer that is closest in meaning to the underlined word. Use prefix/suffix definitions and context clues to help eliminate incorrect answers.

1. The officer quickly became <u>disgruntled</u> after arriving on the scene.
    a. disengaged
    b. upset
    c. envious
    d. careless

2. He had to go through one final <u>evaluation</u> before graduating from the academy.
    a. test
    b. study
    c. grade
    d. choice

3. The thief was clearly <u>bewildered</u> when the officers responded so quickly to the robbery call.
    a. awakened
    b. disturbed
    c. shocked
    d. cranky

4. During a traffic stop the driver continued to <u>exacerbate</u> the situation.
    a. enjoy
    b. digress
    c. worsen
    d. hate

5. He was causing quite the <u>ruckus</u> with his loud music.
    a. crowd
    b. damage
    c. festival
    d. commotion

Answer Explanations

1. B: *Disgruntled*: angry or dissatisfied

Upset: unhappy or disappointed

2. A: *Evaluation*: to make a judgement or assessment

Test: to establish the quality or performance of something

3. C: *Bewildered*: confused or puzzled

Shocked: to cause to feel surprised

4. C: *Exacerbate*: to make a situation worse

Worsen: to make or become worse

5. D: *Ruckus*: a disturbance

Commotion: a state of confused and noisy disturbance

Reading Comprehension

Literary Analysis

Purpose of a Passage

When it comes to an author's writing, readers should always identify a position or stance. No matter how objective a text may seem, readers should assume the author has preconceived beliefs. One can reduce the likelihood of accepting an invalid argument by looking for multiple articles on the topic, including those with varying opinions. If several opinions point in the same direction and are backed by reputable peer-reviewed sources, it's more likely the author has a valid argument. Positions that run contrary to widely-held beliefs and existing data should invite scrutiny. There are exceptions to the rule, so be a careful consumer of information.

Though themes, symbols, and motifs are buried deep within the text and can sometimes be difficult to infer, an **author's purpose** is usually obvious from the beginning. No matter the genre or format, all authors are writing to persuade, inform, entertain, or express feelings. Often, these purposes are blended, with one dominating the rest. It's useful to learn to recognize the author's intent.

Identifying Passage Characteristics

Writing can be classified under four **passage types**: narrative, expository, descriptive, and persuasive. Though these types are not mutually exclusive, one form tends to dominate the rest. By recognizing the type of passage you're reading, you gain insight into *how* you should read. When reading a narrative intended to entertain, sometimes you can read more quickly through the passage if the details are discernible. A technical document, on the other hand, might require a close read, because skimming the passage might cause the reader to miss salient details.

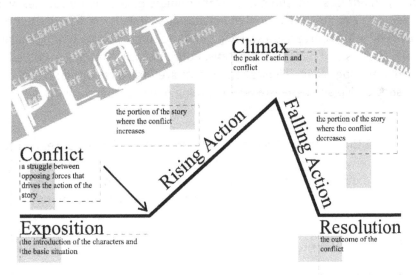

1. **Narrative writing**, at its core, is the art of storytelling. For a narrative to exist, certain elements must be present. First, it must have characters. While many characters are human, characters could be defined as anything that thinks, acts, and talks like a human. For example, many recent movies, such as *Lord of the Rings* and *The Chronicles of Narnia*, include animals, fantasy creatures, and even trees that behave like humans. Narratives also must have a plot or sequence of events. Typically, those events

follow a standard plot diagram, but recent trends start *in medias res* or in the middle of the story. In this instance, foreshadowing and flashbacks often fill in plot details. Finally, along with characters and a plot, there must also be conflict. Conflict is usually divided into two types: internal and external. Internal conflict indicates the character is in turmoil. Think of an angel on one shoulder and the devil on the other, arguing it out. Internal conflicts are presented through the character's thoughts. External conflicts are visible. Types of external conflict include person versus person, person versus nature, person versus technology, person versus the supernatural, or a person versus fate.

2. **Expository writing** is detached and to the point. Since expository writing is designed to instruct or inform, it usually involves directions and steps written in second person ("you" voice) and lacks any persuasive or narrative elements. Sequence words such as *first, second,* and *third,* or *in the first place, secondly,* and *lastly* are often given to add fluency and cohesion. Common examples of expository writing include instructor's lessons, cookbook recipes, and repair manuals.

3. Due to its empirical nature, **technical writing** is filled with steps, charts, graphs, data, and statistics. The goal of technical writing is to advance understanding in a field through the scientific method. Experts such as teachers, doctors, or mechanics use words unique to the profession in which they operate. These words, which often incorporate acronyms, are called **jargon**. Technical writing is a type of expository writing but is not meant to be understood by the general public. Instead, technical writers assume readers have received a formal education in a particular field of study and need no explanation as to what the jargon means. Imagine a doctor trying to understand a diagnostic reading for a car or a mechanic trying to interpret lab results. Only professionals with proper training will fully comprehend the text.

4. **Persuasive writing** is designed to change opinions and attitudes. The topic, stance, and arguments are found in the thesis, positioned near the end of the introduction. Later supporting paragraphs offer relevant quotations, paraphrases, and summaries from primary or secondary sources, which are then interpreted, analyzed, and evaluated. The goal of persuasive writers is not to stack quotes, but to develop original ideas by using sources as a starting point. Good persuasive writing makes powerful arguments with valid sources and thoughtful analysis. Poor persuasive writing is riddled with bias and logical fallacies. Sometimes logical and illogical arguments are sandwiched together in the same text. Therefore, readers should display skepticism when reading persuasive arguments.

Text Structure
Depending on what the author is attempting to accomplish, certain formats or **text structures** work better than others. For example, a sequence structure might work for narration but not when identifying similarities and differences between dissimilar concepts. Similarly, a comparison-contrast structure is not useful for narration. It's the author's job to put the right information in the correct format.

Readers should be familiar with the four main literary structures:

1. **Sequence structure** is when the order of events proceed in a predictable order. In many cases, this means the text goes through the plot elements: exposition, rising action, climax, falling action, and resolution. Readers are introduced to characters, setting, and conflict in the exposition. In the rising action, there's an increase in tension and suspense. The climax is the height of tension and the point of no return. Tension decreases during the falling action. In the resolution, any conflicts presented in the exposition are solved, and the story concludes. An informative text that is structured sequentially will often go in order from one step to the next.

2. In the **problem-solution structure**, authors identify a potential problem and suggest a solution. This form of writing is usually divided into two paragraphs and can be found in informational texts. For example, cell phone, cable, and satellite providers use this structure in manuals to help customers troubleshoot or identify problems with services or products.

3. When authors want to discuss similarities and differences between separate concepts, they arrange thoughts in a **comparison-contrast structure**. Venn diagrams are an effective graphic organizer for comparison-contrast structures, because they feature two overlapping circles that can be used to organize similarities and differences. A comparison-contrast essay organizes one paragraph based on similarities and another based on differences. A comparison-contrast essay can also be arranged with the similarities and differences of individual traits addressed within individual paragraphs. Words such as *however*, *but*, and *nevertheless* help signal a contrast in ideas.

4. Passages that use the **cause and effect structure** are simply asking *why* by demonstrating some type of connection between ideas. Words such as *if*, *since*, *because*, *then*, or *consequently* indicate relationship. By switching the order of a complex sentence, the writer can rearrange the emphasis on different clauses. Saying *If Sheryl is late, we'll miss the dance* is different from saying *We'll miss the dance if Sheryl is late*. One emphasizes Sheryl's tardiness while the other emphasizes missing the dance. Paragraphs can also be arranged in a cause and effect format. Since the format—before and after—is sequential, it is useful when authors wish to discuss the impact of choices. Researchers often apply this paragraph structure to the scientific method.

Point of View

Point of view is an important writing device to consider. In fiction writing, point of view refers to who tells the story or from whose perspective readers are observing as they read. In nonfiction writing, the **point of view** refers to whether the author refers to himself/herself, the readers, or chooses not to mention either. Whether fiction or nonfiction, the author will carefully consider the impact the perspective will have on the purpose and main point of the writing.

- **First-person point of view**: The story is told from the writer's perspective. In fiction, this would mean that the main character is also the narrator. First-person point of view is easily recognized by the use of personal pronouns such as *I*, *me*, *we*, *us*, *our*, *my*, and *myself*.

- **Third-person point of view**: In a more formal essay, this would be an appropriate perspective because the focus should be on the subject matter, not the writer or the reader. Third-person point of view is recognized by the use of the pronouns *he*, *she*, *they*, and *it*. In fiction writing, third person point of view has a few variations.

  - **Third-person limited point of view** refers to a story told by a narrator who has access to the thoughts and feelings of just one character.

  - In **third-person omniscient point of view**, the narrator has access to the thoughts and feelings of all the characters.

  - In **third-person objective point of view**, the narrator is like a fly on the wall and can see and hear what the characters do and say but does not have access to their thoughts and feelings.

- **Second-person point of view**: This point of view isn't commonly used in fiction or non-fiction writing because it directly addresses the reader using the pronouns *you*, *your*, and *yourself*.

Second-person perspective is more appropriate in direct communication, such as business letters or emails.

Point of View	Pronouns Used
First person	I, me, we, us, our, my, myself
Second person	You, your, yourself
Third person	He, she, it, they

Style, Tone, and Mood

Style, tone, and mood are often thought to be the same thing. Though they're closely related, there are important differences to keep in mind. The easiest way to do this is to remember that style "creates and affects" tone and mood. More specifically, style is how the writer uses words to create the desired tone and mood for their writing.

Style

Style can include any number of technical writing choices. A few examples of style choices include:

- **Sentence Construction**: When presenting facts, does the writer use shorter sentences to create a quicker sense of the supporting evidence, or do they use longer sentences to elaborate and explain the information?

- **Technical Language**: Does the writer use jargon to demonstrate their expertise in the subject, or do they use ordinary language to help the reader understand things in simple terms?

- **Formal Language**: Does the writer refrain from using contractions such as *won't* or *can't* to create a more formal tone, or do they use a colloquial, conversational style to connect to the reader?

- **Formatting**: Does the writer use a series of shorter paragraphs to help the reader follow a line of argument, or do they use longer paragraphs to examine an issue in great detail and demonstrate their knowledge of the topic?

On the test, examine the writer's style and how their writing choices affect the way the text comes across.

Tone

Tone refers to the writer's attitude toward the subject matter. Tone is usually explained in terms of a work of fiction. For example, the tone conveys how the writer feels about their characters and the situations in which they're involved. Nonfiction writing is sometimes thought to have no tone at all; however, this is incorrect.

A lot of nonfiction writing has a neutral tone, which is an important tone for the writer to take. A neutral tone demonstrates that the writer is presenting a topic impartially and letting the information speak for itself. On the other hand, nonfiction writing can be just as effective and appropriate if the tone isn't neutral. For instance, take this example involving seat belts:

> Seat belts save more lives than any other automobile safety feature. Many studies show that airbags save lives as well; however, not all cars have airbags. For instance, some older cars don't. Furthermore, air bags aren't entirely reliable. For example, studies show that in 15 percent of accidents airbags don't deploy as designed, but, on the other hand, seat belt malfunctions are extremely rare. The number of highway fatalities has plummeted since laws requiring seat belt usage were enacted.

In this passage, the writer mostly chooses to retain a neutral tone when presenting information. If the writer would instead include their own personal experience of losing a friend or family member in a car accident, the tone would change dramatically. The tone would no longer be neutral and would show that the writer has a personal stake in the content, allowing them to interpret the information in a different way. When analyzing tone, consider what the writer is trying to achieve in the text and how they *create* the tone using style.

Mood

Mood refers to the feelings and atmosphere that the writer's words create for the reader. Like tone, many nonfiction texts can have a neutral mood. To return to the previous example, if the writer would choose to include information about a person they know being killed in a car accident, the text would suddenly carry an emotional component that is absent in the previous example. Depending on how they present the information, the writer can create a sad, angry, or even hopeful mood. When analyzing the mood, consider what the writer wants to accomplish and whether the best choice was made to achieve that end.

Consistency

Whatever style, tone, and mood the writer uses, good writing should remain consistent throughout. If the writer chooses to include the tragic, personal experience above, it would affect the style, tone, and mood of the entire text. It would seem out of place for such an example to be used in the middle of a neutral, measured, and analytical text. To adjust the rest of the text, the writer needs to make additional choices to remain consistent. For example, the writer might decide to use the word *tragedy* in place of the more neutral *fatality*, or they could describe a series of car-related deaths as an *epidemic*. Adverbs and adjectives such as *devastating* or *horribly* could be included to maintain this consistent attitude toward the content. When analyzing writing, look for sudden shifts in style, tone, and mood, and consider whether the writer would be wiser to maintain the prevailing strategy.

Interpret Influences of Historical Context

Studying historical literature is fascinating. It reveals a snapshot in time of people, places, and cultures— a collective set of beliefs and attitudes that no longer exist. Writing changes as attitudes and cultures evolve. Beliefs previously considered immoral or wrong may be considered acceptable today. Researching the historical period of an author gives the reader perspective. The dialogue in Jane Austen's *Pride and Prejudice*, for example, is indicative of social class during the Regency era. Similarly, the stereotypes and slurs in *The Adventures of Huckleberry Finn* were a result of common attitudes and beliefs in the late 1800s, attitudes now found to be reprehensible.

Recognizing Cultural Themes

Regardless of culture, place, or time, certain themes are universal to the human condition. Because humans experience joy, rage, jealousy, and pride, certain themes span centuries. For example, Shakespeare's *Macbeth*, as well as modern works like *The 50th Law* by rapper 50 Cent and Robert Greene or the Netflix series *House of Cards* all feature characters who commit atrocious acts because of ambition. Similarly, *The Adventures of Huckleberry Finn*, published in the 1880s, and *The Catcher in the Rye*, published in the 1950s, both have characters who lie, connive, and survive on their wits.

Moviegoers know whether they are seeing an action, romance or horror film, and are often disappointed if the movie doesn't fit into the conventions of a particular category. Similarly, categories or genres give readers a sense of what to expect from a text. Some of the most basic genres in literature include books, short stories, poetry, and drama. Many genres can be split into sub-genres. For example, the sub-genres of historical fiction, realistic fiction, and fantasy all fit under the fiction genre.

Each genre has a unique way of approaching a particular theme. Books and short stories use plot, characterization, and setting, while poems rely on figurative language, sound devices, and symbolism. Dramas reveal plot through dialogue and the actor's voice and body language.

Main Ideas and Supporting Details

It is very important to know the difference between the topic and the main idea of the text. Even though these two are similar because they both present the central point of a text, they have distinctive differences. A **topic** is the subject of the text; it can usually be described in a one- to two-word phrase and appears in the simplest form. On the other hand, the **main idea** is more detailed and provides the author's central point of the text. It can be expressed through a complete sentence and can be found in the beginning, middle, or end of a paragraph. In most nonfiction books, the first sentence of the passage usually (but not always) states the main idea. Take a look at the passage below to review the topic versus the main idea.

Cheetahs

Cheetahs are one of the fastest mammals on land, reaching up to 70 miles an hour over short distances. Even though cheetahs can run as fast as 70 miles an hour, they usually only have to run half that speed to catch up with their choice of prey. Cheetahs cannot maintain a fast pace over long periods of time because they will overheat their bodies. After a chase, cheetahs need to rest for approximately 30 minutes prior to eating or returning to any other activity.

In the example above, the topic of the passage is "Cheetahs" simply because that is the subject of the text. The main idea of the text is "Cheetahs are one of the fastest mammals on land but can only maintain this fast pace for short distances." While it covers the topic, it is more detailed and refers to the text in its entirety. The text continues to provide additional details called supporting details, which will be discussed in the next section.

Supporting Details

Supporting details help readers better develop and understand the main idea. Supporting details answer questions like *who, what, where, when, why,* and *how.* Different types of supporting details include examples, facts and statistics, anecdotes, and sensory details.

Persuasive and informative texts often use supporting details. In persuasive texts, authors attempt to make readers agree with their point of view, and supporting details are often used as "selling points." If authors make a statement, they should support the statement with evidence in order to adequately persuade readers. Informative texts use supporting details such as examples and facts to inform readers. Take another look at the previous "Cheetahs" passage to find examples of supporting details.

Cheetahs

Cheetahs are one of the fastest mammals on land, reaching up to 70 miles an hour over short distances. Even though cheetahs can run as fast as 70 miles an hour, they usually only have to run half that speed to catch up with their choice of prey. Cheetahs cannot maintain a fast pace over long periods of time because they will overheat their bodies. After a chase, cheetahs need to rest for approximately 30 minutes prior to eating or returning to any other activity.

In the example above, supporting details include:

- Cheetahs reach up to 70 miles per hour over short distances.
- They usually only have to run half that speed to catch up with their prey.
- Cheetahs will overheat their bodies if they exert a high speed over longer distances.
- Cheetahs need to rest for 30 minutes after a chase.

Drawing Conclusions

Drawing conclusions requires being an active reader, as a reader must make a prediction and analyze facts to identify a conclusion. There are a few ways to determine a logical conclusion, but careful reading is the most important. It's helpful to read a passage a few times, noting details that seem important to the piece. A reader should also identify key words in a passage to determine the logical conclusion or determination that flows from the information presented.

Textual evidence within the details helps readers draw a conclusion about a passage. **Textual evidence** refers to information—facts and examples that support the main point. Textual evidence will likely come from outside sources and can be in the form of quoted or paraphrased material. In order to draw a conclusion from evidence, it's important to examine the credibility and validity of that evidence as well as how (and if) it relates to the main idea.

If an author presents a differing opinion or a counterargument in order to refute it, the reader should consider how and why this information is being presented. It is meant to strengthen the original argument and shouldn't be confused with the author's intended conclusion, but it should also be considered in the reader's final evaluation.

Sometimes, authors explicitly state the conclusion they want readers to understand. Alternatively, a conclusion may not be directly stated. In that case, readers must rely on the implications to form a logical conclusion:

On the way to the bus stop, Michael realized his homework wasn't in his backpack. He ran back to the house to get it and made it back to the bus just in time.

In this example, though it's never explicitly stated, it can be inferred that Michael is a student on his way to school in the morning. When forming a conclusion from implied information, it's important to read the text carefully to find several pieces of evidence in the text to support the conclusion.

Readers should pay attention to the **sequence**, or the order in which details are laid out in the text, as this can be important to understanding its meaning as a whole. Writers will often use transitional words to help the reader understand the order of events and to stay on track. Words like *next, then, after*, and *finally* show that the order of events is important to the author. In some cases, the author omits these transitional words, and the sequence is implied. Authors may even purposely present the information out of order to make an impact or have an effect on the reader. An example might be when a narrative writer uses **flashback** to reveal information.

There are several ways readers can draw conclusions from authors' ideas, such as note taking, text evidence, text credibility, writing a response to text, directly stated information versus implications, outlining, summarizing, and paraphrasing. Let's take a look at each important strategy to help readers draw logical conclusions.

Note Taking

When readers take notes throughout texts or passages, they are jotting down important facts or points that the author makes. **Note taking** is a useful record of information that helps readers understand the text or passage and respond to it. When taking notes, readers should keep lines brief and filled with pertinent information so that they are not rereading a large amount of text, but rather just key points, elements, or words. After readers have completed a text or passage, they can refer to their notes to help them form a conclusion about the author's ideas in the text or passage.

Text Evidence

Text evidence is the information readers find in a text or passage that supports the main idea or point(s) in a story. In turn, text evidence can help readers draw conclusions about the text or passage. The information should be taken directly from the text or passage and placed in quotation marks. Text evidence provides readers with information to support ideas about the text so that they do not rely simply on their own thoughts. Details should be precise, descriptive, and factual. Statistics are a great piece of text evidence because they provide readers with exact numbers and not just a generalization. For example, instead of saying "Asia has a larger population than Europe," authors could provide detailed information such as, "In Asia there are over 4 billion people, whereas in Europe there are a little over 750 million." More definitive information provides better evidence to readers to help support their conclusions about texts or passages.

Text Credibility

Credible sources are important when drawing conclusions because readers need to be able to trust what they are reading. Authors should always use credible sources to help gain the trust of their readers. A text is **credible** when it is believable and the author is objective and unbiased. If readers do not trust an author's words, they may simply dismiss the text completely. For example, if an author writes a persuasive essay, he or she is outwardly trying to sway readers' opinions to align with their own. Readers may agree or disagree with the author, which may, in turn, lead them to believe that the author is credible or not credible. Also, readers should keep in mind the source of the text. If readers review a journal about astronomy, would a more reliable source be a NASA employee or a medical doctor? Overall, text credibility is important when drawing conclusions, because readers want reliable sources that support the decisions they have made about the author's ideas.

Writing a Response to Text

Once readers have determined their opinions and validated the credibility of a text, they can then reflect on the text. Writing a response to a text is one way readers can reflect on the given text or

passage. When readers write responses to a text, it is important for them to rely on the evidence within the text to support their opinions or thoughts. Supporting evidence such as facts, details, statistics, and quotes directly from the text are key pieces of information readers should reflect upon or use when writing a response to text.

Directly Stated Information Versus Implications

Engaged readers should constantly self-question while reviewing texts to help them form conclusions. Self-questioning is when readers review a paragraph, page, passage, or chapter and ask themselves, "Did I understand what I read?," "What was the main event in this section?," "Where is this taking place?," and so on. Authors can provide clues or pieces of evidence throughout a text or passage to guide readers toward a conclusion. This is why active and engaged readers should read the text or passage in its entirety before forming a definitive conclusion. If readers do not gather all the pieces of evidence needed, then they may jump to an illogical conclusion.

At times, authors directly state conclusions while others simply imply them. Of course, it is easier if authors outwardly provide conclusions to readers, because it does not leave any information open to interpretation. On the other hand, implications are things that authors do not directly state but can be assumed based off of information they provided. If authors only imply what may have happened, readers can form a menagerie of ideas for conclusions. For example, look at the following statement: "Once we heard the sirens, we hunkered down in the storm shelter." In this statement, the author does not directly state that there was a tornado, but clues such as "sirens" and "storm shelter" provide insight to the readers to help form that conclusion.

Outlining

An **outline** is a system used to organize writing. When reading texts, outlining is important because it helps readers organize important information in a logical pattern using roman numerals. Usually, outlines start with the main idea(s) and then branch out into subgroups or subsidiary thoughts of subjects. Not only do outlines provide a visual tool for readers to reflect on how events, characters, settings, or other key parts of the text or passage relate to one another, but they can also lead readers to a stronger conclusion.

The sample below demonstrates what a general outline looks like.

I. Main Topic 1
    a. Subtopic 1
    b. Subtopic 2
        1. Detail 1
        2. Detail 2
II. Main Topic 2
    a. Subtopic 1
    b. Subtopic 2
        1. Detail 1
        2. Detail 2

Summarizing

Summarizing is when readers determine what is important throughout the text or passage and rewrite a shortened version of the material in their own words. A summary should identify the main idea of the text or passage. Important details or supportive evidence should also be accurately reported in the summary. If writers provide irrelevant details in the summary, it may cloud the greater meaning of the summary in the text. When summarizing, writers should not include their opinions, quotes, or what they thought the author should have said. A clear summary provides clarity of the text or passage to the readers.

Paraphrasing

Another strategy readers can use to help them fully comprehend a text or passage is paraphrasing. **Paraphrasing** is when readers take the author's words and put them into their own words. When readers and writers paraphrase, they should avoid copying the text—that is plagiarism. It is also important to include as many details as possible when restating the facts. Not only will this help readers and writers recall information, but by putting the information into their own words, they demonstrate whether or not they fully comprehend the text or passage. Look at the example below showing an original text and how to paraphrase it.

> *Original Text*: Fenway Park is home to the beloved Boston Red Sox. The stadium opened on April 20, 1912. The stadium currently seats over 37,000 fans, many of whom travel from all over the country to experience the iconic team and nostalgia of Fenway Park.

> *Paraphrased*: On April 20, 1912, Fenway Park opened. Home to the Boston Red Sox, the stadium now seats over 37,000 fans. Many spectators travel to watch the Red Sox and experience the spirit of Fenway Park.

Paraphrasing, summarizing, and quoting can often cross paths with one another. Review the chart below showing the similarities and differences between the three strategies.

Paraphrasing	Summarizing	Quoting
Uses own words	Puts main ideas into own words	Uses words that are identical to text
References original source	References original source	Requires quotation marks
Uses own sentences	Shows important ideas of source	Uses author's own words and ideas

Inferences in a Text

Readers should be able to make inferences. **Making an inference** requires the reader to read between the lines and look for what is implied rather than what is directly stated. That is, using information that

is known from the text, the reader is able to make a logical assumption about information that is *not* directly stated but is probably true. Read the following passage:

"Hey, do you wanna meet my new puppy?" Jonathan asked.

"Oh, I'm sorry but please don't—" Jacinta began to protest, but before she could finish, Jonathan had already opened the passenger side door of his car and a perfect white ball of fur came bouncing towards Jacinta.

"Isn't he the cutest?" beamed Jonathan.

"Yes—achoo!—he's pretty—aaaachooo!!—adora—aaa—aaaachoo!" Jacinta managed to say in between sneezes. "But if you don't mind, I—I—achoo!—need to go inside."

Which of the following can be inferred from Jacinta's reaction to the puppy?
a. She hates animals.
b. She is allergic to dogs.
c. She prefers cats to dogs.
d. She is angry at Jonathan.

An inference requires the reader to consider the information presented and then form their own idea about what is probably true. Based on the details in the passage, what is the best answer to the question? Important details to pay attention to include the tone of Jacinta's dialogue, which is overall polite and apologetic, as well as her reaction itself, which is a long string of sneezes. Answer choices (a) and (d) both express strong emotions ("hates" and "angry") that are not evident in Jacinta's speech or actions. Answer choice (c) mentions cats, but there is nothing in the passage to indicate Jacinta's feelings about cats. Answer choice (b), "she is allergic to dogs," is the most logical choice—based on the fact that she began sneezing as soon as a fluffy dog approached her, it makes sense to guess that Jacinta might be allergic to dogs. So even though Jacinta never directly states, "Sorry, I'm allergic to dogs!" using the clues in the passage, it is still reasonable to guess that this is true.

Making inferences is crucial for readers of literature because literary texts often avoid presenting complete and direct information to readers about characters' thoughts or feelings, or they present this information in an unclear way, leaving it up to the reader to interpret clues given in the text. In order to make inferences while reading, readers should ask themselves:

- What details are being presented in the text?
- Is there any important information that seems to be missing?
- Based on the information that the author *does* include, what else is probably true?
- Is this inference reasonable based on what is already known?

Apply Information

A natural extension of being able to make an inference from a given set of information is also being able to apply that information to a new context. This is especially useful in nonfiction or informative writing. Considering the facts and details presented in the text, readers should consider how the same information might be relevant in a different situation. The following is an example of applying an inferential conclusion to a different context:

Often, individuals behave differently in large groups than they do as individuals. One example of this is the psychological phenomenon known as the bystander effect. According to the bystander effect, the more people who witness an accident or crime occur, the less likely each individual bystander is to respond or offer assistance to the victim. A classic example of this is the murder of Kitty Genovese in New York City in the 1960s. Although there were over thirty witnesses to her killing by a stabber, none of them intervened to help Kitty or contact the police.

Considering the phenomenon of the bystander effect, what would probably happen if somebody tripped on the stairs in a crowded subway station?
    a. Everybody would stop to help the person who tripped
    b. Bystanders would point and laugh at the person who tripped
    c. Someone would call the police after walking away from the station
    d. Few if any bystanders would offer assistance to the person who tripped

This question asks readers to apply the information they learned from the passage, which is an informative paragraph about the bystander effect. According to the passage, this is a concept in psychology that describes the way people in groups respond to an accident—the more people are present, the less likely any one person is to intervene. While the passage illustrates this effect with the example of a woman's murder, the question asks readers to apply it to a different context—in this case, someone falling down the stairs in front of many subway passengers. Although this specific situation is not discussed in the passage, readers should be able to apply the general concepts described in the paragraph. The definition of the bystander effect includes any instance of an accident or crime in front of a large group of people. The question asks about a situation that falls within the same definition, so the general concept should still hold true: in the midst of a large crowd, few individuals are likely to actually respond to an accident. In this case, answer choice (d) is the best response.

Critical Thinking Skills

It's important to read any piece of writing critically. The goal is to discover the point and purpose of what the author is writing about through analysis. It's also crucial to establish the point or stance the author has taken on the topic of the piece. After determining the author's perspective, readers can then more effectively develop their own viewpoints on the subject of the piece.

It is important to distinguish between **fact and opinion** when reading a piece of writing. A fact is information that can be proven true. If information can be disproved, it is not a fact. For example, water freezes at or below thirty-two degrees Fahrenheit. An argument stating that water freezes at seventy degrees Fahrenheit cannot be supported by data and is therefore not a fact. Facts tend to be associated with science, mathematics, and statistics. Opinions are information open to debate. Opinions are often tied to subjective concepts like equality, morals, and rights. They can also be controversial.

Authors often use words like *think, feel, believe,* or *in my opinion* when expressing opinion, but these words won't always appear in an opinion piece, especially if it is formally written. An author's opinion may be backed up by facts, which gives it more credibility, but that opinion should not be taken as fact. A critical reader should be suspect of an author's opinion, especially if it is only supported by other opinions.

Fact	Opinion
There are 9 innings in a game of baseball.	Baseball games run too long.
James Garfield was assassinated on July 2, 1881.	James Garfield was a good president.
McDonalds has stores in 118 countries.	McDonalds has the best hamburgers.

Critical readers examine the facts used to support an author's argument. They check the facts against other sources to be sure those facts are correct. They also check the validity of the sources used to be sure those sources are credible, academic, and/or peer-reviewed. Consider that when an author uses another person's opinion to support their argument, even if it is an expert's opinion, it is still only an opinion and should not be taken as fact. A strong argument uses valid, measurable facts to support ideas. Even then, the reader may disagree with the argument as it may be rooted in their personal beliefs.

An authoritative argument may use the facts to sway the reader. In the example of global warming, many experts differ in their opinions of what alternative fuels can be used to aid in offsetting it. Because of this, a writer may choose to only use the information and expert opinion that supports his or her viewpoint.

If the argument is that wind energy is the best solution, the author will use facts that support this idea. That same author may leave out relevant facts on solar energy. The way the author uses facts can influence the reader, so it's important to consider the facts being used, how those facts are being presented, and what information might be left out.

Critical readers should also look for errors in the argument such as logical fallacies and bias. A **logical fallacy** is a flaw in the logic used to make the argument. Logical fallacies include slippery slope, straw man, and begging the question. Authors can also reflect **bias** if they ignore an opposing viewpoint or present their side in an unbalanced way. A strong argument considers the opposition and finds a way to refute it. Critical readers should look for an unfair or one-sided presentation of the argument and be skeptical, as a bias may be present. Even if this bias is unintentional, if it exists in the writing, the reader should be wary of the validity of the argument.

Readers should also look for the use of **stereotypes**, which refer to specific groups. Stereotypes are often negative connotations about a person or place and should always be avoided. When a critical reader finds stereotypes in a piece of writing, they should immediately be critical of the argument and consider the validity of anything the author presents. Stereotypes reveal a flaw in the writer's thinking and may suggest a lack of knowledge or understanding about the subject.

Author's Use of Language

Authors utilize a wide range of techniques to tell a story or communicate information. Readers should be familiar with the most common of these techniques. Techniques of writing are also commonly known as **rhetorical devices**.

Types of Appeals

In nonfiction writing, authors employ argumentative techniques to present their opinion to readers in the most convincing way. First of all, persuasive writing usually includes at least one type of appeal: an appeal to logic (logos), emotion (pathos), or credibility and trustworthiness (ethos). When a writer appeals to logic, they are asking readers to agree with them based on research, evidence, and an established line of reasoning. An author's argument might also appeal to readers' emotions, perhaps by including personal stories and anecdotes (a short narrative of a specific event). A final type of appeal, appeal to authority, asks the reader to agree with the author's argument on the basis of their expertise or credentials. Consider three different approaches to arguing the same opinion:

Logic (Logos)

This is an example of an appeal to logic, or **logos**:

> Our school should abolish its current ban on cell phone use on campus. This rule was adopted last year as an attempt to reduce class disruptions and help students focus more on their lessons. However, since the rule was enacted, there has been no change in the number of disciplinary problems in class. Therefore, the rule is ineffective and should be done away with.

The author uses evidence to disprove the logic of the school's rule (the rule was supposed to reduce discipline problems; the number of problems has not been reduced; therefore, the rule is not working) and call for its repeal.

Emotion (Pathos)

An author's argument might also appeal to readers' emotions, perhaps by including personal stories and anecdotes. The next example presents an appeal to emotion, or **pathos**. By sharing the personal anecdote of one student and speaking about emotional topics like family relationships, the author invokes the reader's empathy in asking them to reconsider the school rule.

> Our school should abolish its current ban on cell phone use on campus. If they aren't able to use their phones during the school day, many students feel isolated from their loved ones. For example, last semester, one student's grandmother had a heart attack in the morning. However, because he couldn't use his cell phone, the student didn't know about his grandmother's accident until the end of the day—when she had already passed away and it was too late to say goodbye. By preventing students from contacting their friends and family, our school is placing undue stress and anxiety on students.

Credibility (Ethos)

Finally, an appeal to authority, or **ethos**, includes a statement from a relevant expert. In this case, the author uses a doctor in the field of education to support the argument. All three examples begin from the same opinion—the school's phone ban needs to change—but rely on different argumentative styles to persuade the reader.

> Our school should abolish its current ban on cell phone use on campus. According to Dr. Bartholomew Everett, a leading educational expert, "Research studies show that cell phone usage has no real impact on student attentiveness. Rather, phones provide a valuable technological resource for learning. Schools need to learn how to integrate this new technology into their curriculum." Rather than banning phones altogether, our school should follow the advice of experts and allow students to use phones as part of their learning.

Rhetorical Questions

Another commonly used argumentative technique is asking **rhetorical questions**, questions that do not actually require an answer but that push the reader to consider the topic further.

> I wholly disagree with the proposal to ban restaurants from serving foods with high sugar and sodium contents. Do we really want to live in a world where the government can control what we eat? I prefer to make my own food choices.

Here, the author's rhetorical question prompts readers to put themselves in a hypothetical situation and imagine how they would feel about it.

Figurative Language

Literary texts also employ rhetorical devices. **Figurative language** like simile and metaphor is a type of rhetorical device commonly found in literature. In addition to rhetorical devices that play on the meanings of words, there are also rhetorical devices that use the sounds of words. These devices are most often found in poetry but may also be found in other types of literature and in nonfiction writing like speech texts.

Alliteration and assonance are both varieties of sound repetition. Other types of sound repetition include: anaphora, repetition that occurs at the beginning of the sentences; epiphora, repetition occurring at the end of phrases; antimetabole, repetition of words in reverse order; and antiphrasis, a form of denial of an assertion in a text.

Alliteration refers to the repetition of the first sound of each word. Recall Robert Burns' opening line:

My love is like a red, red rose

This line includes two instances of alliteration: "love" and "like" (repeated *L* sound), as well as "red" and "rose" (repeated *R* sound). Next, **assonance** refers to the repetition of vowel sounds, and can occur anywhere within a word. Here is the opening of a poem by John Keats: ·

When I have fears that I may cease to be

Before my pen has glean'd my teeming brain

Assonance can be found in the words "fears," "cease," "be," "glean'd," and "teeming," all of which stress the long *E* sound. Both alliteration and assonance create a harmony that unifies the writer's language.

Another sound device is **onomatopoeia**, or words whose spelling mimics the sound they describe. Words such as "crash," "bang," and "sizzle" are all examples of onomatopoeia. Use of onomatopoetic language adds auditory imagery to the text.

Readers are probably most familiar with the technique of pun. A **pun** is a play on words, taking advantage of two words that have the same or similar pronunciation. Puns can be found throughout Shakespeare's plays, for instance:

Now is the winter of our discontent

Made glorious summer by this son of York

These lines from *Richard III* contain a play on words. Richard III refers to his brother, the newly crowned King Edward IV, as the "son of York," referencing their family heritage from the house of York. However, while drawing a comparison between the political climate and the weather (times of political trouble were the "winter," but now the new king brings "glorious summer"), Richard's use of the word "son" also implies another word with the same pronunciation, "sun"—so Edward IV is also like the sun, bringing light, warmth, and hope to England. Puns are a clever way for writers to suggest two meanings at once.

Practice Questions

The next question is based on the following conversation between a scientist and a politician.

> Scientist: Last year was the warmest ever recorded in the last 134 years. During that time period, the ten warmest years have all occurred since 2000. This correlates directly with the recent increases in carbon dioxide as large countries like China, India, and Brazil continue developing and industrializing. No longer do just a handful of countries burn massive amounts of carbon-based fossil fuels; it is quickly becoming the case throughout the whole world as technology and industry spread.

> Politician: Yes, but there is no causal link between increases in carbon emissions and increasing temperatures. The link is tenuous and nothing close to certain. We need to wait for all of the data before drawing hasty conclusions. For all we know, the temperature increase could be entirely natural. I believe the temperatures also rose dramatically during the dinosaurs' time, and I do not think they were burning any fossil fuels back then.

1. What is one point on which the scientist and politician agree?
   a. Burning fossil fuels causes global temperatures to rise.
   b. Global temperatures are increasing.
   c. Countries must revisit their energy policies before it's too late.
   d. Earth's climate naturally goes through warming and cooling periods.

The next question is based on the following passage.

> A famous children's author recently published a historical fiction novel under a pseudonym; however, it did not sell as many copies as her children's books. In her earlier years, she had majored in history and earned a graduate degree in Antebellum American History, which is the time frame of her new novel. Critics praised this newest work far more than the children's series that made her famous. In fact, her new novel was nominated for the prestigious Albert J. Beveridge Award but still isn't selling like her children's books, which fly off the shelves because of her name alone.

2. Which one of the following statements might be accurately inferred based on the above passage?
   a. The famous children's author produced an inferior book under her pseudonym.
   b. The famous children's author is the foremost expert on Antebellum America.
   c. The famous children's author did not receive the bump in publicity for her historical novel that it would have received if it were written under her given name.
   d. People generally prefer to read children's series than historical fiction.

The next three questions are based on the following passage.

> Smoking tobacco products is terribly destructive. A single cigarette contains over 4,000 chemicals, including 43 known carcinogens and 400 deadly toxins. Some of the most dangerous ingredients include tar, carbon monoxide, formaldehyde, ammonia, arsenic, and DDT. Smoking can cause numerous types of cancer including throat, mouth, nasal cavity, esophageal, gastric, pancreatic, renal, bladder, and cervical cancer.

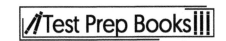

Cigarettes contain a drug called nicotine, one of the most addictive substances known to man. Addiction is defined as a compulsion to seek the substance despite negative consequences. According to the National Institute of Drug Abuse, nearly 35 million smokers expressed a desire to quit smoking in 2015; however, more than 85 percent of those who struggle with addiction will not achieve their goal. Almost all smokers regret picking up that first cigarette. You would be wise to learn from their mistake if you have not yet started smoking.

According to the U.S. Department of Health and Human Services, 16 million people in the United States presently suffer from a smoking-related condition and nearly nine million suffer from a serious smoking-related illness. According to the Centers for Disease Control and Prevention (CDC), tobacco products cause nearly six million deaths per year. This number is projected to rise to over eight million deaths by 2030. Smokers, on average, die ten years earlier than their nonsmoking peers.

In the United States, local, state, and federal governments typically tax tobacco products, which leads to high prices. Nicotine users who struggle with addiction sometimes pay more for a pack of cigarettes than for a few gallons of gas. Additionally, smokers tend to stink. The smell of smoke is all-consuming and creates a pervasive nastiness. Smokers also risk staining their teeth and fingers with yellow residue from the tar.

Smoking is deadly, expensive, and socially unappealing. Clearly, smoking is not worth the risks.

3. Which of the following statements most accurately summarizes the passage?
   a. Tobacco is less healthy than many alternatives.
   b. Tobacco is deadly, expensive, and socially unappealing, and smokers would be much better off kicking the addiction.
   c. In the United States, local, state, and federal governments typically tax tobacco products, which leads to high prices.
   d. Tobacco products shorten smokers' lives by ten years and kill more than six million people per year.

4. The author would be most likely to agree with which of the following statements?
   a. Smokers should only quit cold turkey and avoid all nicotine cessation devices.
   b. Other substances are more addictive than tobacco.
   c. Smokers should quit for whatever reason that gets them to stop smoking.
   d. People who want to continue smoking should advocate for a reduction in tobacco product taxes.

5. Which of the following represents an opinion statement on the part of the author?
   a. According to the Centers for Disease Control and Prevention (CDC), tobacco products cause nearly six million deaths per year.
   b. Nicotine users who struggle with addiction sometimes pay more for a pack of cigarettes than a few gallons of gas.
   c. They also risk staining their teeth and fingers with yellow residue from the tar.
   d. Additionally, smokers tend to stink. The smell of smoke is all-consuming and creates a pervasive nastiness.

Answer Explanations

1. B: The scientist and politician largely disagree, but the question asks for a point where the two are in agreement. The politician would not concur that burning fossil fuels causes global temperatures to rise; thus, Choice A is incorrect. The politician also would not agree with Choice C suggesting that countries must revisit their energy policies. By inference from the given information, the scientist would likely not concur that earth's climate naturally goes through warming and cooling cycles; so Choice D is incorrect. However, both the scientist and politician would agree that global temperatures are increasing. The reason for this is in dispute. The politician thinks it is part of the earth's natural cycle; the scientist thinks it is from the burning of fossil fuels. However, both acknowledge an increase, so Choice B is the correct answer.

2. C: We are looking for an inference—a conclusion that is reached on the basis of evidence and reasoning—from the passage that will likely explain why the famous children's author did not achieve her usual success with the new genre (despite the book's acclaim). Choice A is incorrect because the statement is false according to the passage. Choice B is incorrect because, although the passage says the author has a graduate degree on the subject, it would be an unrealistic leap to infer that she is the foremost expert on Antebellum America. Choice D is incorrect because there is nothing in the passage to lead us to infer that people generally prefer a children's series to historical fiction. In contrast, Choice C can be logically inferred since the passage speaks of the great success of the children's series and the declaration that the fame of the author's name causes the children's books to "fly off the shelves." Thus, she did not receive any bump from her name since she published the historical novel under a pseudonym, and Choice C is correct.

3. B: The author is clearly opposed to tobacco. He cites disease and deaths associated with smoking. He points to the monetary expense and aesthetic costs. Choice A is incorrect because alternatives to smoking are not even addressed in the passage. Choice C is incorrect because it does not summarize the passage but rather is just a premise. Choice D is incorrect because, while these statistics are a premise in the argument, they do not represent a summary of the piece. Choice B is the correct answer because it states the three critiques offered against tobacco and expresses the author's conclusion.

4. C: We are looking for something the author would agree with, so it will almost certainly be anti-smoking or an argument in favor of quitting smoking. Choice A is incorrect because the author does not speak against means of cessation. Choice B is incorrect because the author does not reference other substances but does speak of how addictive nicotine, a drug in tobacco, is. Choice D is incorrect because the author certainly would not encourage reducing taxes to encourage a reduction of smoking costs, thereby helping smokers to continue the habit. Choice C is correct because the author is definitely attempting to persuade smokers to quit smoking.

5. D: Here, we are looking for an opinion of the author's rather than a fact or statistic. Choice A is incorrect because quoting statistics from the Centers of Disease Control and Prevention is stating facts, not opinions. Choice B is incorrect because it expresses the fact that cigarettes sometimes cost more than a few gallons of gas. It would be an opinion if the author said that cigarettes were not affordable. Choice C is incorrect because yellow stains are a known possible adverse effect of smoking. Choice D is correct as an opinion because smell is subjective. Some people might like the smell of smoke, they might not have working olfactory senses, and/or some people might not find the smell of smoke akin to "pervasive nastiness," so this is the expression of an opinion. Thus, Choice D is the correct answer.

Mathematics

Arithmetic

Addition with Whole Numbers and Fractions
Addition combines two quantities together. With whole numbers, this is taking two sets of things and merging them into one, then counting the result. For example, $4 + 3 = 7$. When adding numbers, the order does not matter: $3 + 4 = 7$ also works. Longer lists of whole numbers can be added together. The result of adding numbers is called the **sum**.

With fractions, the number on top is the **numerator**, and the number on the bottom is the **denominator**. To add fractions, the denominator must be the same—a **common denominator**. To find a common denominator, the existing numbers on the bottom must be considered, and the lowest number they will both multiply into must be determined. Consider the following equation:

$$\frac{1}{3} + \frac{5}{6} = ?$$

The numbers 3 and 6 both multiply into 6. Three can be multiplied by 2, and 6 can be multiplied by 1. The top and bottom of each fraction must be multiplied by the same number. Then, the numerators are added together to get a new numerator. The following equation is the result:

$$\frac{1}{3} + \frac{5}{6} = \frac{2}{6} + \frac{5}{6} = \frac{7}{6}$$

Subtraction with Whole Numbers and Fractions
Subtraction is taking one quantity away from another, so it is the opposite of addition. The expression $4 - 3$ means taking 3 away from 4. So, $4 - 3 = 1$. In this case, the order matters, since it entails taking one quantity away from the other, rather than just putting two quantities together. The result of subtraction is also called the **difference**.

To subtract fractions, the denominator must be the same. Then, subtract the numerators together to get a new numerator. Here is an example:

$$\frac{1}{3} - \frac{5}{6} = \frac{2}{6} - \frac{5}{6} = \frac{-3}{6} = -\frac{1}{2}$$

Multiplication with Whole Numbers and Fractions
Multiplication is a kind of repeated addition. The expression 4×5 is taking four sets, each of them having five things in them, and putting them all together. That means $4 \times 5 = 5 + 5 + 5 + 5 = 20$. As with addition, the order of the numbers does not matter. The result of a multiplication problem is called the **product**.

To multiply fractions, the numerators are multiplied to get the new numerator, and the denominators are multiplied to get the new denominator:

$$\frac{1}{3} \times \frac{5}{6} = \frac{1 \times 5}{3 \times 6} = \frac{5}{18}$$

When multiplying fractions, common factors can cancel or divide into one another, when factors appear in the numerator of one fraction and the denominator of the other fraction. Here is an example:

$$\frac{1}{3} \times \frac{9}{8} = \frac{1}{1} \times \frac{3}{8} = 1 \times \frac{3}{8} = \frac{3}{8}$$

The numbers 3 and 9 have a common factor of 3, so that factor can be divided out.

Division with Whole Numbers and Fractions

Division is the opposite of multiplication. With whole numbers, it means splitting up one number into sets of equal size. For example, $16 \div 8$ is the number of sets of eight things that can be made out of sixteen things. Thus, $16 \div 8 = 2$. As with subtraction, the order of the numbers will make a difference in division. The answer to a division problem is called the **quotient**, while the number in front of the division sign is called the *dividend*, and the number behind the division sign is called the **divisor**.

To divide fractions, the first fraction must be multiplied with the reciprocal of the second fraction. The **reciprocal** of the fraction $\frac{x}{y}$ is the fraction $\frac{y}{x}$. Here is an example:

$$\frac{1}{3} \div \frac{5}{6} = \frac{1}{3} \times \frac{6}{5}$$

$$\frac{6}{15} = \frac{2}{5}$$

Recognizing Equivalent Fractions and Mixed Numbers

The value of a fraction does not change if multiplying or dividing both the numerator and the denominator by the same number (other than 0). In other words, $\frac{x}{y} = \frac{a \times x}{a \times y} = \frac{x \div a}{y \div a}$, as long as a is not 0. This means that $\frac{2}{5} = \frac{4}{10}$, for example. If x and y are integers that have no common factors, then the fraction is said to be **simplified**. This means $\frac{2}{5}$ is simplified, but $\frac{4}{10}$ is not.

Often when working with fractions, the fractions need to be rewritten so that they all share a single denominator—this is called finding a common denominator for the fractions. Using two fractions, $\frac{a}{b}$ and $\frac{c}{d}$, the numerator and denominator of the left fraction can be multiplied by d, while the numerator and denominator of the right fraction can be multiplied by b. This provides the fractions $\frac{a \times d}{b \times d}$ and $\frac{c \times b}{d \times b}$ with the common denominator $b \times d$.

A fraction whose numerator is smaller than its denominator is called a **proper fraction**. A fraction whose numerator is bigger than its denominator is called an **improper fraction**. These numbers can be rewritten as a combination of integers and fractions, called a **mixed number**. For example, $\frac{6}{5} = \frac{5}{5} + \frac{1}{5} = 1 + \frac{1}{5}$, and can be written as $1\frac{1}{5}$.

Estimating

Estimation is finding a value that is close to a solution but is not the exact answer. For example, if there are values in the thousands to be multiplied, then each value can be estimated to the nearest thousand and the calculation performed. This value provides an approximate solution that can be determined very quickly.

Recognition of Decimals

The **decimal system** is a way of writing out numbers that uses ten different numerals: 0, 1, 2, 3, 4, 5, 6, 7, 8, and 9. This is also called a "base ten" or "base 10" system. Other bases are also used. For example, computers work with a base of 2. This means they only use the numerals 0 and 1.

The **decimal place** denotes how far to the right of the decimal point a numeral is. The first digit to the right of the decimal point is in the *tenths* place. The next is the *hundredths*. The third is the *thousandths*.

So, 3.142 has a 1 in the tenths place, a 4 in the hundredths place, and a 2 in the thousandths place.

The **decimal point** is a period used to separate the *ones* place from the *tenths* place when writing out a number as a decimal.

A **decimal number** is a number written out with a decimal point instead of as a fraction, for example, 1.25 instead of $\frac{5}{4}$. Depending on the situation, it can sometimes be easier to work with fractions and sometimes easier to work with decimal numbers.

A decimal number is **terminating** if it stops at some point. It is called **repeating** if it never stops, but repeats a pattern over and over. It is important to note that every rational number can be written as a terminating decimal or as a repeating decimal.

Addition with Decimals

To add decimal numbers, each number in columns needs to be lined up by the decimal point. For each number being added, the zeros to the right of the last number need to be filled in so that each of the numbers has the same number of places to the right of the decimal. Then, the columns can be added together. Here is an example of $2.45 + 1.3 + 8.891$ written in column form:

$$2.450$$

$$1.300$$

$$+\ 8.891$$

Zeros have been added in the columns so that each number has the same number of places to the right of the decimal.

Added together, the correct answer is 12.641:

$$2.450$$

$$1.300$$

$$+\ 8.891$$

$$12.641$$

Subtraction with Decimals

Subtracting decimal numbers is the same process as adding decimals. Here is $7.89 - 4.235$ written in column form:

$$7.890$$

$$\underline{-\ 4.235}$$

$$3.655$$

A zero has been added in the column so that each number has the same number of places to the right of the decimal.

Multiplication with Decimals

Decimals can be multiplied as if there were no decimal points in the problem. For example, 0.5×1.25 can be rewritten and multiplied as 5×125, which equals 625.

The final answer will have the same number of decimal points as the total number of decimal places in the problem. The first number has one decimal place, and the second number has two decimal places. Therefore, the final answer will contain three decimal places:

$$0.5 \times 1.25 = 0.625$$

Division with Decimals

Dividing a decimal by a whole number entails using long division first by ignoring the decimal point. Then, the decimal point is moved the number of places given in the problem.

For example, $6.8 \div 4$ can be rewritten as $68 \div 4$, which is 17. There is one non-zero integer to the right of the decimal point, so the final solution would have one decimal place to the right of the solution. In this case, the solution is 1.7.

Dividing a decimal by another decimal requires changing the divisor to a whole number by moving its decimal point. The decimal place of the dividend should be moved by the same number of places as the divisor. Then, the problem is the same as dividing a decimal by a whole number.

For example, $5.72 \div 1.1$ has a divisor with one decimal point in the denominator. The expression can be rewritten as $57.2 \div 11$ by moving each number one decimal place to the right to eliminate the decimal. The long division can be completed as $572 \div 11$ with a result of 52. Since there is one non-zero integer to the right of the decimal point in the problem, the final solution is 5.2.

In another example, $8 \div 0.16$ has a divisor with two decimal points in the denominator. The expression can be rewritten as $800 \div 16$ by moving each number two decimal places to the right to eliminate the decimal in the divisor. The long division can be completed with a result of 50.

Fraction and Percent Equivalencies

The word **percent** comes from the Latin phrase for "per one hundred." A percent is a way of writing out a fraction. It is a fraction with a denominator of 100. Thus, $65\% = \frac{65}{100}$.

To convert a fraction to a percent, the denominator is written as 100. For example:

$$\frac{3}{5} = \frac{60}{100} = 60\%$$

In converting a percent to a fraction, the percent is written with a denominator of 100, and the result is simplified. For example:

$$30\% = \frac{30}{100} = \frac{3}{10}$$

Percent Problems

The basic percent equation is the following:

$$\frac{is}{of} = \frac{\%}{100}$$

The placement of numbers in the equation depends on what the question asks.

Example 1

Find 40% of 80.

Basically, the problem is asking, "What is 40% of 80?" The 40% is the percent, and 80 is the number to find the percent "of." The equation is:

$$\frac{x}{80} = \frac{40}{100}$$

Solving the equation by cross-multiplication, the problem becomes:

$$100x = 80(40)$$

Solving for x gives the answer: $x = 32$.

Example 2

What percent of 100 is 20?

The 20 fills in the "is" portion, while 100 fills in the "of." The question asks for the percent, so that will be x, the unknown. The following equation is set up:

$$\frac{20}{100} = \frac{x}{100}$$

Cross-multiplying yields the equation $100x = 20(100)$. Solving for x gives the answer of 20%.

Example 3
30% of what number is 30?

The following equation uses the clues and numbers in the problem:

$$\frac{30}{x} = \frac{30}{100}$$

Cross-multiplying results in the equation $30(100) = 30x$. Solving for *x* gives the answer $x = 100$.

Problems Involving Estimation

Estimation is finding a value that is close to a solution, but is not the exact answer. For example, if there are values in the thousands to be multiplied, then each value can be estimated to the nearest thousand and the calculation performed. This value provides an approximate solution that can be determined very quickly.

Rounding is the process of bumping a number up or down, based on a specified place value. First, the place value is specified. Then, the digit to its right is looked at. For example, if rounding to the nearest hundreds place, the digit in the tens place is used. If it is a 0, 1, 2, 3, or 4, the digit being rounded to is left alone. If it is a 5, 6, 7, 8 or 9, the digit being rounded to is increased by one. All other digits before the decimal point are then changed to zeros, and the digits in decimal places are dropped. If a decimal place is being rounded to, all subsequent digits are just dropped. For example, if 845,231.45 was to be rounded to the nearest thousands place, the answer would be 845,000. The 5 would remain the same due to the 2 in the hundreds place. Also, if 4.567 was to be rounded to the nearest tenths place, the answer would be 4.6. The 5 increased to 6 due to the 6 in the hundredths place, and the rest of the decimal is dropped.

Sometimes when performing operations such as multiplying numbers, the result can be estimated by rounding. For example, to estimate the value of 11.2×2.01, each number can be rounded to the nearest integer. This will yield a result of 22.

Rounding numbers helps with estimation because it changes the given number to a simpler, although less accurate, number than the exact given number. Rounding allows for easier calculations, which estimate the results of using the exact given number. The accuracy of the estimate and ease of use depends on the place value to which the number is rounded. Rounding numbers consists of:

- Determining what place value the number is being rounded to
- Examining the digit to the right of the desired place value to decide whether to round up or keep the digit, and
- Replacing all digits to the right of the desired place value with zeros.

To round 746,311 to the nearest ten thousand, the digit in the ten thousands place should be located first. In this case, this digit is 4 (74<u>6</u>,311). Then, the digit to its right is examined. If this digit is 5 or greater, the number will be rounded up by increasing the digit in the desired place by one. If the digit to the right of the place value being rounded is 4 or less, the number will be kept the same. For the given example, the digit being examined is a 6, which means that the number will be rounded up by increasing the digit to the left by one. Therefore, the digit 4 is changed to a 5. Finally, to write the rounded number, any digits to the left of the place value being rounded remain the same and any to its right are replaced with zeros. For the given example, rounding 746,311 to the nearest ten thousand will produce 750,000. To round 746,311 to the nearest hundred, the digit to the right of the three in the hundreds place is

examined to determine whether to round up or keep the same number. In this case, that digit is a 1, so the number will be kept the same and any digits to its right will be replaced with zeros. The resulting rounded number is 746,300.

Rounding place values to the right of the decimal follows the same procedure, but digits being replaced by zeros can simply be dropped. To round 3.752891 to the nearest thousandth, the desired place value is located (3.752891) and the digit to the right is examined. In this case, the digit 8 indicates that the number will be rounded up, and the 2 in the thousandths place will increase to a 3. Rounding up and replacing the digits to the right of the thousandths place produces 3.753000 which is equivalent to 3.753. Therefore, the zeros are not necessary and the rounded number should be written as 3.753.

When rounding up, if the digit to be increased is a 9, the digit to its left is increased by 1 and the digit in the desired place value is changed to a zero. For example, the number 1,598 rounded to the nearest ten is 1,600. Another example shows the number 43.72961 rounded to the nearest thousandth is 43.730 or 43.73.

Rate, Percent, and Measurement Problems

A **ratio** compares the size of one group to the size of another. For example, there may be a room with 4 tables and 24 chairs. The ratio of tables to chairs is 4:24. Such ratios behave like fractions in that both sides of the ratio by the same number can be multiplied or divided. Thus, the ratio 4:24 is the same as the ratio 2:12 and 1:6.

One quantity is **proportional** to another quantity if the first quantity is always some multiple of the second. For instance, the distance travelled in five hours is always five times to the speed as travelled. The distance is proportional to speed in this case.

One quantity is **inversely proportional** to another quantity if the first quantity is equal to some number divided by the second quantity. The time it takes to travel one hundred miles will be given by 100 divided by the speed travelled. The time is inversely proportional to the speed.

When dealing with word problems, there is no fixed series of steps to follow, but there are some general guidelines to use. It is important that the quantity to be found is identified. Then, it can be determined how the given values can be used and manipulated to find the final answer.

Example 1
Jana wants to travel to visit Alice, who lives one hundred and fifty miles away. If she can drive at fifty miles per hour, how long will her trip take?

The quantity to find is the *time* of the trip. The time of a trip is given by the distance to travel divided by the speed to be traveled. The problem determines that the distance is one hundred and fifty miles, while the speed is fifty miles per hour. Thus, 150 divided by 50 is $150 \div 50 = 3$. Because *miles* and *miles per hour* are the units being divided, the miles cancel out. The result is 3 hours.

Example 2
Bernard wishes to paint a wall that measures twenty feet wide by eight feet high. It costs ten cents to paint one square foot. How much money will Bernard need for paint?

The final quantity to compute is the *cost* to paint the wall. This will be ten cents ($0.10) for each square foot of area needed to paint. The area to be painted is unknown, but the dimensions of the wall are given; thus, it can be calculated.

The dimensions of the wall are 20 feet wide and 8 feet high. Since the area of a rectangle is length multiplied by width, the area of the wall is $8 \times 20 = 160$ square feet. Multiplying 0.1×160 yields \$16 as the cost of the paint.

The **average** or **mean** of a collection of numbers is given by adding those numbers together and then dividing by the total number of values. A **weighted average** or **weighted mean** is given by adding the numbers multiplied by their weights, then dividing by the sum of the weights:

$$\frac{w_1 x_1 + w_2 x_2 + w_3 x_3 \ldots + w_n x_n}{w_1 + w_2 + w_3 + \cdots + w_n}$$

An **ordinary average** is a weighted average where all the weights are 1.

Solving for X in Proportions

Proportions are commonly used to solve word problems to find unknown values such as x that are some percent or fraction of a known number. Proportions are solved by cross-multiplying and then dividing to arrive at x. The following examples show how this is done:

1) $\frac{75\%}{90\%} = \frac{25\%}{x}$

To solve for x, the fractions must be cross multiplied:

$$(75\% x = 90\% \times 25\%)$$

To make things easier, let's convert the percentages to decimals:

$$(0.9 \times 0.25 = 0.225 = 0.75x)$$

To get rid of x's co-efficient, each side must be divided by that same coefficient to get the answer $x = 0.3$. The question could ask for the answer as a percentage or fraction in lowest terms, which are 30% and $\frac{3}{10}$, respectively.

2) $\frac{x}{12} = \frac{30}{96}$

Cross-multiply: $96x = 30 \times 12$
Multiply: $96x = 360$
Divide: $x = 360 \div 96$
Answer: $x = 3.75$

3) $\frac{0.5}{3} = \frac{x}{6}$

Cross-multiply: $3x = 0.5 \times 6$
Multiply: $3x = 3$
Divide: $x = 3 \div 3$
Answer: $x = 1$

You may have noticed there's a faster way to arrive at the answer. If there is an obvious operation being performed on the proportion, the same operation can be used on the other side of the proportion to solve for x. For example, in the first practice problem, 75% became 25% when divided by 3, and upon doing the same to 90%, the correct answer of 30% would have been found with much less legwork.

However, these questions aren't always so intuitive, so it's a good idea to work through the steps, even if the answer seems apparent from the outset.

Word Problems

Word problems can appear daunting, but don't let the verbiage psych you out. No matter the scenario or specifics, the key to answering them is to translate the words into a math problem. Always keep in mind what the question is asking and what operations could lead to that answer.

Translating Words into Math

In order to translate a word problem into an expression, look for a series of key words indicating addition, subtraction, multiplication, or division:

Addition: *add, altogether, together, plus, increased by, more than, in all, sum*, and *total*

Subtraction: *minus, less than, difference, decreased by, fewer than, remain*, and *take away*

Multiplication: *times, twice, of, double*, and *triple*

Division: *divided by, cut up, half, quotient of, split*, and *shared equally*

Identifying and utilizing the proper units for the scenario requires knowing how to apply the conversion rates for money, length, volume, and mass. For example, given a scenario that requires subtracting 8 inches from $2\frac{1}{2}$ feet, both values should first be expressed in the same unit (they could be expressed $\frac{2}{3}$ft and $2\frac{1}{2}$ft, or 8in and 30in). The desired unit for the answer may also require converting back to another unit.

Consider the following scenario: A parking area along the river is only wide enough to fit one row of cars and is $\frac{1}{2}$ kilometers long. The average space needed per car is 5 meters. How many cars can be parked along the river? First, all measurements should be converted to similar units: $\frac{1}{2}$km = 500m. The operation(s) needed should be identified. Because the problem asks for the number of cars, the total space should be divided by the space per car. 500 meters divided by 5 meters per car yields a total of 100 cars. Written as an expression, the meters unit cancels and the cars unit is left: $\frac{500m}{5m/car}$ the same as $500m \times \frac{1\ car}{5m}$ yields 100 cars.

When dealing with problems involving elapsed time, breaking the problem down into workable parts is helpful. For example, suppose the length of time between 1:15pm and 3:45pm must be determined. From 1:15pm to 2:00pm is 45 minutes (knowing there are 60 minutes in an hour). From 2:00pm to 3:00pm is 1 hour. From 3:00pm to 3:45pm is 45 minutes. The total elapsed time is 45 minutes plus 1 hour plus 45 minutes. This sum produces 1 hour and 90 minutes. 90 minutes is over an hour, so this is converted to 1 hour (60 minutes) and 30 minutes. The total elapsed time can now be expressed as 2 hours and 30 minutes.

Example 1

Alexandra made $96 during the first 3 hours of her shift as a temporary worker at a law office. She will continue to earn money at this rate until she finishes in 5 more hours. How much does Alexandra make per hour? How much will Alexandra have made at the end of the day?

The hourly rate can be figured by dividing $96 by 3 hours to get $32 per hour. Now her total pay can be figured by multiplying $32 per hour by 8 hours, which comes out to $256.

Example 2
Bernard wishes to paint a wall that measures 20 feet wide by 8 feet high. It costs $0.10 to paint 1 square foot. How much money will Bernard need for paint?

The final quantity to compute is the *cost* to paint the wall. This will be ten cents ($0.10) for each square foot of area needed to paint. The area to be painted is unknown, but the dimensions of the wall are given; thus, it can be calculated.

The dimensions of the wall are 20 feet wide and 8 feet high. Since the area of a rectangle is length multiplied by width, the area of the wall is $8 \times 20 = 160$ square feet. Multiplying 0.1×160 yields $16 as the cost of the paint.

Basic Geometry

Calculating Perimeter and Area
There are many key facts related to geometry that are applicable. The sum of the measures of the angles of a triangle are 180°, and for a quadrilateral, the sum is 360°. Rectangles and squares each have four right angles. A **right angle** has a measure of 90°.

Perimeter
The **perimeter** is the distance around a figure or the sum of all sides of a polygon.

The formula for the perimeter of a square is four times the length of a side. For example, the following square has side lengths of 5 feet:

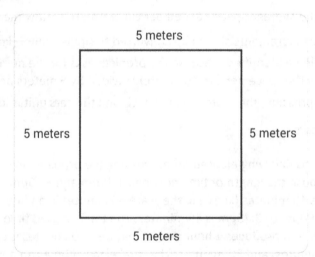

The perimeter is 20 feet because 4 times 5 is 20.

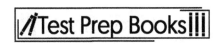

The formula for a perimeter of a rectangle is the sum of twice the length and twice the width. For example, if the length of a rectangle is 10 inches and the width 8 inches, then the perimeter is 36 inches because:

$$P = 2l + 2w = 2(10) + 2(8)$$

$$20 + 16 = 36 \text{ inches}$$

Area

The **area** is the amount of space inside of a figure, and there are formulas associated with area.

The area of a triangle is the product of one-half the base and height. For example, if the base of the triangle is 2 feet and the height 4 feet, then the area is 4 square feet. The following equation shows the formula used to calculate the area of the triangle:

$$A = \frac{1}{2}bh = \frac{1}{2}(2)(4) = 4 \text{ square feet}$$

The area of a square is the length of a side squared, and the area of a rectangle is length multiplied by the width. For example, if the length of the square is 7 centimeters, then the area is 49 square centimeters. The formula for this example is $A = s^2 = 7^2 = 49$ square centimeters. An example is if the rectangle has a length of 6 inches and a width of 7 inches, then the area is 42 square inches:

$$A = lw = 6(7) = 42 \text{ square inches}$$

The area of a trapezoid is ½ the height times the sum of the bases. For example, if the length of the bases are 2.5 and 3 feet and the height 3.5 feet, then the area is 9.625 square feet. The following formula shows how the area is calculated:

$$A = \frac{1}{2}h(b_1 + b_2) = \frac{1}{2}(3.5)(2.5 + 3)$$

$$\frac{1}{2}(3.5)(5.5) = 9.625 \text{ square feet}$$

The perimeter of a figure is measured in single units, while the area is measured in square units.

Applying Mathematics Concepts to Law-Enforcement Scenarios

Calculating the Cost of Stolen Goods

A common application of arithmetic found on the Police Officer Entrance Exam is to calculate the cost of stolen goods. Performing operations with monetary values typically involves decimals, so test takers must be comfortable fluidly adding, subtracting, multiplying, and dividing with decimals. Consider the following example:

A police officer receives a call from a local jeweler about a break-in that occurred overnight. When taking stock of the damages, the jeweler reported the following:

- 1 broken window: $375
- 2 smashed display cases: $254.95 each
- 5 stolen tennis bracelets: $120.85 each

- 3 amethyst pendants: $68.23 each
- 6 ruby pendants: $70.79 each
- 12 rings: $108.42 each
- 2 diamond necklaces: $899.99 each

What was the total assessed value of the damages and stolen goods?

To calculate the total sum, the totals for each item need to be calculated and then added together.

- 1 broken window: $375
- 2 smashed display cases: $254.95 × 2 = $509.90
- 5 stolen tennis bracelets: $120.85 × 5 = $604.25
- 3 amethyst pendants: $68.23 × 3 = 204.69
- 6 ruby pendants: $70.79 × 6 = $424.74
- 12 rings: $108.42 × 12 = $1301.04
- 2 diamond necklaces: $899.99 × 2 = $1799.98

$Total = \$375 + \$509.90 + \$604.25 + \$204.69 + \$424.74 + \$1301.04 + \$1799.98 = \$5219.60$

Practice Questions

1. 3.4+2.35+4=
    a. 5.35
    b. 9.2
    c. 9.75
    d. 10.25

2. $5.88 \times 3.2 =$
    a. 18.816
    b. 16.44
    c. 20.352
    d. 17

3. $\frac{3}{25} =$
    a. 0.15
    b. 0.1
    c. 0.9
    d. 0.12

4. Which of the following is largest?
    a. 0.45
    b. 0.096
    c. 0.3
    d. 0.313

5. Which of the following is NOT a way to write 40 percent of N?
    a. $(0.4)N$

    b. $\frac{2}{5}N$

    c. $40N$

    d. $\frac{4N}{10}$

Answer Explanations

1. C: The decimal points are lined up, with zeroes put in as needed. Then, the numbers are added just like integers:

$$
\begin{array}{r}
3.40 \\
2.35 \\
+4.00 \\
\hline
9.75
\end{array}
$$

2. A: This problem can be multiplied as 588×32, except at the end, the decimal point needs to be moved three places to the left. Performing the multiplication will give 18,816 and moving the decimal place over three places results in 18.816.

3. D: The fraction is converted so that the denominator is 100 by multiplying the numerator and denominator by 4, to get $\frac{3}{25} = \frac{12}{100}$. Dividing a number by 100 just moves the decimal point two places to the left, with a result of 0.12.

4. A: Figure out which is largest by looking at the first non-zero digits. Choice *B*'s first non-zero digit is in the hundredths place. The other three all have non-zero digits in the tenths place, so it must be *A*, *C*, or *D*. Of these, *A* has the largest first non-zero digit.

5. C: 40*N* would be 4000% of *N*. It's possible to check that each of the others is actually 40% of *N*.

Grammar

To prepare for the Police Offer Exam, it's helpful to review the parts of speech to see how they collectively function to form complete sentences.

The Eight Parts of Speech		
Nouns	refer to people, places, things, or ideas	*mother, school, book, beauty*
Pronouns	alternatives for nouns	*I, you, she, it, this*
Verbs	express action or states of being	*run, drive, appear, remember*
Adjectives	modify nouns	*dark blue, average*
Adverbs	modify verbs; answer *when? where? how?* and *why?*	*soon, there, happily, entirely*
Prepositions	express the relationship between a noun and another element	*about, before, through, after*
Coordinating conjunctions	used to connect clauses or sentences or to coordinate words in the same clause	*and, but, for, yet, nor, so*
Interjections	exclamations	*Wow! Hi!*

Nouns

A **noun** is a word used to describe a person, place, thing, or idea. They are often the subject, object, or direct object of a sentence. There are five main types of nouns:

- Common nouns
- Proper nouns
- General nouns
- Specific nouns
- Collective nouns

Common nouns are general words that can be used to name people, places, and things:

- People: mom, brother, neighbor
- Places: office, gym, restaurant
- Things: bed, computer, sandwich

Proper nouns are specific words that can be used to name people, places, and things. For example:

- People: Amelia Earhart, Albert Einstein, Stephen Hawking
- Places: Philadelphia, Pennsylvania; Bombay, India; Australia
- Brands: Levi's jeans, Apple computer

Note the difference between common and proper nouns:

- Common noun: The suspect said that she'd eaten breakfast with her sister that morning.
- Proper noun: The suspect said that she'd eaten breakfast with Jane Lowe that morning.

Sometimes common and proper nouns appear in the same sentence:

George Washington was the first *president*.

General nouns are words used to describe conditions or ideas. They are abstract by nature. For example:

- Condition: bravery, love
- Idea: justice, freedom

Specific nouns are words used to describe particular people, places, and things. For example:

- People: victim, perpetrator, officer
- Places: city, beach, stadium
- Things: holster, badge, custody

Collective nouns are words used to refer to groups of people, places, or things as a whole. For example, *flock, group, bunch, crowd, tribe,* and *pack* are all collective nouns.

Pronouns

A **pronoun** is a word that replaces a noun in a sentence. There are seven types:

- Personal
- Reflexive
- Relative
- Interrogative
- Demonstrative
- Indefinite
- Reciprocal

Personal pronouns are words that represent specific people or things (for example, *I, you, he, she, me, you,* and *mine*).

Three things must be considered in choosing the correct personal pronoun: grammatical case, quantity, and point of view.

Reflexive pronouns are preceded by the adverb, adjective, pronoun, or noun to which they refer. They are used to rename the subjects of action verbs or function as different types of objects: *myself, himself, herself, themselves, yourself, yourselves, ourselves.*

> She was in a hurry, so she did the reports *herself*.

Intensive pronouns are reflexive pronouns that are only used to add emphasis to the subject of a sentence. They aren't required for meaning: *myself, yourself, himself, herself, itself, ourselves, yourselves,* and *themselves*.

> We met the king *himself*.

Relative pronouns are used to connect phrases or clauses to a noun or pronoun. There are eight relative pronouns: *that, which, who, whom, whose, whichever, whoever,* and *whomever*.

> The first point of entry was closed, *which* meant we had to enter through the back.

Interrogative pronouns are used to ask a question. There are five interrogative pronouns: *what, which, who, whom,* and *whose.*

> *Whose* boots are those?

Special note about *who/whom*: substitute *he* for *who* and *him* for *whom* to determine which should be used.

> [*Who* or *whom*] wrote that email?

> He wrote that email?

> Him wrote that email?

He=who, so *who* is correct.

> She gave the presentation to [*who* or *whom*]?

> She gave the presentation to he?

> She gave the presentation to him?

Him=whom, so *whom* is correct.

Demonstrative pronouns take the place of a noun phrase. There are six demonstrative pronouns: *this, that, these, those, none,* and *neither.*

> *That* is not the right thing to do.

Indefinite Pronouns

Indefinite pronouns are used when referring to a person or thing in a general way. Some examples include *all, another, any, anyone, each, everything, nobody,* and *several.*

> *Each* is separated by category.

Reciprocal pronouns are used when two or more people have done something simultaneously. The two reciprocal pronouns are: *each other* and *one another.*

> They were kind to *each other.*

Verbs

Verbs are words that express actions or occurrences; they signal the sentence's predicate (what the subject is doing). While a noun is often the subject of a sentence, the verb expresses what is happening or what has happened. For a sentence to be complete, a verb must be included. There are three main types of verbs: *action, linking,* and *helping.*

Action Verbs

Action verbs are verbs that show that something is happening, or that something/someone is in possession of something else.

> Security personnel *detained* the prisoner.

> Detective Suarez *has* a subject in custody.

There are two types of action verbs: transitive and intransitive.

Transitive verbs refer to an object that is receiving the action. There must be a direct object.

> The sergeant apprehended the suspect.

The transitive verb in this sentence is *apprehended. The suspect* is the verb's direct object, or that which receives the action. Without the direct object to go along with the transitive verb, the sentence wouldn't make sense: *the sergeant apprehended.* Transitive verbs can be active or passive:

A verb is active if the subject of the sentence performs the action. **Transitive active verbs** are the verbs in sentences with direct objects.

> Officer Lee *pursued* the suspect.

The subject, *Officer Lee*, performed the action, *pursued*, and *the suspect* is the direct object that receives that action.

Transitive passive verbs are when the subject or direct object is on the receiving end of the action.

> The suspect *was pursued* by Officer Lee.

In this sentence, the subject of the sentence is *the suspect* and it is receiving Officer Lee's action.

Intransitive verbs are action words that don't need direct objects.

> The recruits *progressed* well.

The verb in this sentence is *progressed*. We know it is an intransitive verb because a direct object (what they progressed in or with) is unnecessary for the sentence to be complete.

Linking Verbs

Linking verbs are verbs that link the subject of the sentence to more information about that subject.

> The altercation *was* verbal.

In this sentence, *the altercation* is the subject, and we learn something new about it—*what kind* of altercation it was. *Was* serves as the verb in this sentence, linking the subject and the added information.

Common Linking Verbs			
is	are	seems	feels
was	become	might	am

Some action verbs can also be linking verbs.

> The defendant *appeared* before the court.

In the sentence above, *appeared* is an action verb.

> The defendant *appeared remorseful* when addressing the judge.

In the sentence above, *appeared* links the defendant to the subject complement, *remorseful.*

Helping Verbs

Helping verbs are words that appear before action or linking verbs. Their purpose is to add information about either time or possibility. The addition of a helping verb to an action or linking verb creates a verb phrase.

> Andrew *is appearing* before the judge.

In this sentence, *Andrew* is the subject, *is* is the helping verb, and *appearing* is the action verb.

Common Helping Verbs			
am	is	are	was
were	be	being	been
have	has	had	do
does	did	done	could
should	would	can	might

Conjugation

Conjugation refers to changing verbs to indicate *point of view, number, tense,* and *mood.* It also refers to subject/verb agreement. Verbs are conjugated to match the point of view of the subject of a sentence.

> I *am* a police officer.

In this sentence, *am* is a conjugation of the verb *to be,* for the subject *I. I to be a police officer,* or *I are a police officer,* are incorrect.

Number

Verbs are conjugated to indicate how many people are involved in the action of a sentence.

> She *runs* a ten-minute mile.

> They *run* every day.

The verb *to run* is conjugated by adding an *s* to indicate that one person is running. If the action includes more than one person, the conjugation changes: an *s* is not needed.

<u>Tense</u>

The tense of a verb indicates when the action is taking place. There are six possible verb tenses:

- Present: The action is currently happening or happens habitually.
- Past: The action has happened already.
- Future: The action will happen at a later date.
- Present perfect: The action started in the past and continues.
- Past perfect: Two actions occurred in the past, one before the other.
- Future perfect: The action will be complete before another action occurs in the future.

Conjugating a verb so that it is in the present or past tense is as simple as changing the form through letter addition or substitution. For the other tenses, including future, present perfect, past perfect, and future perfect, a helping verb is required.

Present: I run.   *Present perfect*: I have run.

Past: I ran.   *Past perfect*: I had run.

Future: I will run.   *Future perfect*: I will have run.

Adjectives

An **adjective** is a word used to modify or describe a noun or pronoun. By answering questions about the noun or pronoun, adjectives make a sentence more specific. An adjective usually answers one of three questions:

- Which one?

    The *older* brother was seen entering the building.

    In this sentence, the *brother* is the subject. The adjective, *older*, tells us which one.

- What kind?

    Professional officers can become detectives.

    In this sentence, the adjective, *professional,* tells us what kind of officer can become a detective.

- How many or how often?

    She drinks milk *five* times a day.

    In this sentence, the adjective, *five*, tells us how many times a day the person drinks milk.

<u>Comparisons</u>

Adjectives can also be used to make comparisons. These adjectives come in two forms: relative and absolute.

Relative adjectives show a comparison between two things. There are three degrees of relative adjectives: positive, comparative, and superlative.

- **Positive**: the base form of the adjective

  The painting was *beautiful.*

- **Comparative**: a higher level of some quality of the adjective

  The painting was *more* beautiful than I expected it to be.

- **Superlative**: The highest form of quality of the adjective

  The painting was the *most beautiful* painting I've ever seen.

Absolute adjectives also show comparison, but not in varying degrees; they're non-gradable. A good example of an absolute adjective is *empty.* If there are two boxes, and one of them is *empty,* the other box cannot be *emptier, more emptier,* or *most empty.* The box is either empty or it is not. *Empty* is an absolute adjective.

Articles

Articles are used to identify a noun in a sentence. There are three articles in the English language: *the, a,* and *an. The* is a **definite article,** and *a* and *an* are **indefinite articles,** so it's important to choose the right one for meaning.

The is used when there is a limited number (definite) of something being referred to.

> I left *the book* on the couch.

In this sentence, the noun being referred to is *book.* Choosing the article *the* indicates that one particular book was left on the couch.

A and *an* are used when there is not a fixed amount (indefinite) of something being referred to.

> I left *a book* on the couch.

Again, the noun in the sentence is *book.* The article changed to *a* because the sentence no longer refers to one specific book.

On the test, it will be important to remember that *an* comes before nouns that begin with a vowel.

> I left *an old* book on the couch.

Adverbs

An **adverb** is a word or phrase that modifies verbs, adjectives, or other adverbs. Like adjectives, adverbs are also words that can be used to answer questions. Adverbs answer the following:

- When? She drove *yesterday.*
- Where? They drove *here.*
- How? He drove *quickly.*
- To what extent? She drives *whenever possible.*
- Why? We ride the bus *to avoid traffic.*

As seen in the examples, some adverbs end in *–ly*, but not all. The words *not* and *never* are considered adverbs because they modify adjectives.

Again, like adjectives, adverbs can be used to make comparisons in three degrees: positive, comparative, and superlative.

- They *quietly* went into the building.
- The squad went into the building *more quietly* than the cadets.
- The squad leader went into the building *most quietly.*

Prepositions

A **preposition** is a word that appears in a sentence to show the relationship between a noun or pronoun and another element.

> The books are *on* the shelves.

The preposition, *on*, shows the relationship between the books (noun) and the shelves (another noun).

Common Prepositions				
aboard	behind	during	outside	to
about	below	for	over	toward
above	beyond	inside	past	under
among	by	into	since	upon
around	despite	near	through	within

Conjunctions

Conjunctions join pieces of words, phrases, or clauses. There are three types of conjunctions: coordinating, correlative, and subordinating.

Coordinating conjunctions connect equal parts of sentences. Common coordinating conjunctions are *for, and, nor, but, or, yet, so* (sometimes called the FANBOYS).

> The poem was brief, *but* it was beautiful.

In this sentence, *but* connects two independent clauses into one sentence.

In some cases, coordinating conjunctions convey a sense of contrast. In the example above, the poem's beauty is in contrast to the length of it.

Correlative conjunctions show the connection between pairs. Common correlative conjunctions are *either/or, neither/nor, not only/but also, both/and, whether/or,* and *so/as.*

> *Either* you're having lunch at home, *or* you're eating out.

In this sentence, *either* and *or* are used to connect two options.

Subordinating conjunctions join dependent clauses with independent clauses, providing a transition between two ideas. This transition often adds information about time, place, or the effect of something.

> Our team lost the game *because* Jim was unprepared.

In this sentence, *because* is connecting two clauses and indicating a cause and effect relationship between them.

Common Subordinating Conjunctions		
after	since	whenever
although	so that	where
because	unless	wherever
before	when	in order that

Interjections

An **interjection** is an exclamatory word used to indicate extreme emotion or feeling. Some examples include *Hey! Oh!* and *Wow!*

These words can be used alone as a complete sentence, or they can be added to a sentence to indicate a forceful change in thought or add feeling.

> *Wow!* You look great today!

> *Hey*, in my opinion, he deserves the presidency.

In the first sentence, *Wow!* is the interjection used to add feeling to the speaker's opinion. In the second sentence, the speaker uses *Hey* to grab the listener's attention before expressing their opinion.

Types of Sentences

There isn't an overabundance of absolutes in grammar, but here is one: every sentence in the English language falls into one of four categories.

- **Declarative**: a simple statement that ends with a period

  The price of milk per gallon is the same as the price of gasoline.

- **Imperative**: a command, instruction, or request that ends with a period

  Buy milk when you stop to fill up your car with gas.

- **Interrogative**: a question that ends with a question mark

  Will you buy the milk?

- **Exclamatory**: a statement or command that expresses emotions like anger, urgency, or surprise and ends with an exclamation mark

  Buy the milk now!

Declarative sentences are the most common type, probably because they are comprised of the most general content, without any of the bells and whistles that the other three types contain. They are, simply, declarations or statements of any degree of seriousness, importance, or information.

Imperative sentences often seem to be missing a subject. The subject is there, though; it is just not visible or audible because it is implied. Look at the imperative example sentence.

> Buy the milk when you fill up your car with gas.

You is the implied subject, the one to whom the command is issued. This is sometimes called *the understood you* because it is understood that *you* is the subject of the sentence.

Interrogative sentences—those that ask questions—are defined as such from the idea of the word *interrogation*, the action of questions being asked of suspects by investigators. Although that is serious business, interrogative sentences apply to all kinds of questions.

To exclaim is at the root of exclamatory sentences. These are made with strong emotions behind them. The only technical difference between a declarative or imperative sentence and an exclamatory one is the exclamation mark at the end. The example declarative and imperative sentences can both become an exclamatory one simply by putting an exclamation mark at the end of the sentences.

> The price of milk per gallon is the same as the price of gasoline!

> Buy milk when you stop to fill up your car with gas!

After all, someone might be really excited by the price of gas or milk, or they could be mad at the person that will be buying the milk! However, as stated before, exclamation marks in abundance defeat their own purpose! After a while, they begin to cause fatigue! When used only for their intended purpose, they can have their expected and desired effect.

Subjects

Every sentence must include a subject and a verb. The **subject** of a sentence is who or what the sentence is about. It's often directly stated and can be determined by asking "Who?" or "What?" did the action:

Most sentences contain a direct subject, in which the subject is mentioned in the sentence.

> *Kelly mowed the lawn.*

> Who mowed the lawn? *Kelly*

> *The air-conditioner ran all night.*

> What ran all night? *the air-conditioner*

The subject of imperative sentences is *you*, because imperative subjects are commands. the subject is implied because it is a command:

> *Go home after the meeting.*

> Who should go home after the meeting? *you* (implied)

In expletive sentences that start with "there are" or "there is," the subject is found after the predicate. The subject cannot be "there," so it must be another word in the sentence:

There is a cup sitting on the coffee table.

What is sitting on the coffee table? *a cup*

Simple and Complete Subjects

A **complete subject** includes the simple subject and all the words modifying it, including articles and adjectives. A **simple subject** is the single noun without its modifiers.

A warm, chocolate-chip cookie sat on the kitchen table.

Complete subject: *a warm, chocolate-chip cookie*

Simple subject: *cookie*

The words *a, warm, chocolate,* and *chip* all modify the simple subject *cookie.*

There might also be a **compound subject**, which would be two or more nouns without the modifiers.

A little girl and her mother walked into the shop.

Complete subject: *A little girl and her mother*

Compound subject: *girl, mother*

In this case, *the girl and her mother* are both completing the action of walking into the shop, so this is a compound subject.

Subject-Verb Agreement

The subject of a sentence and its verb must agree. The cornerstone rule of **subject-verb agreement** is that subject and verb must agree in number. Whether the subject is singular or plural, the verb must follow suit.

Incorrect: The *houses is* new.

Correct: The *houses are* new.

Also Correct: The *house is* new.

In other words, a singular subject requires a singular verb, and a plural subject requires a plural verb. The words or phrases that come between the subject and verb do not alter this rule.

Incorrect: The *houses* built of brick *is* new.

Correct: The *houses* built of brick *are* new.

Incorrect: The *houses* with the sturdy porches *is* new.

Correct: The *houses* with the sturdy porches *are* new.

73

The subject will always follow the verb when a sentence begins with *here* or *there.* Identify these with care.

>Incorrect: Here *is* the *houses* with sturdy porches.

>Correct: Here *are* the *houses* with sturdy porches.

The subject in the sentences above is not *here*, it is *houses*. Remember, *here* and *there* are never subjects. Be careful that contractions such as *here's* or *there're* do not cause confusion!

Two subjects joined by *and* require a plural verb form, except when the two combine to make one thing:

>Incorrect: *Garrett and Jonathan is* over there.

>Correct: *Garrett and Jonathan are* over there.

>Incorrect: *Spaghetti and meatballs are* a delicious meal!

>Correct: *Spaghetti and meatballs is* a delicious meal!

In the example above, *spaghetti and meatballs* is a compound noun. However, *Garrett and Jonathan* is not a compound noun.

Two singular subjects joined by *or, either/or,* or *neither/nor* call for a singular verb form.

>Incorrect: *Butter or syrup are* acceptable.

>Correct: *Butter or syrup is* acceptable.

Plural subjects joined by *or, either/or*, or *neither/nor* are, indeed, plural.

>The *chairs or the boxes are* being moved next.

If one subject is singular and the other is plural, the verb should agree with the closest noun.

>Correct: The *chair or the boxes are* being moved next.

>Correct: The *chairs or the box is* being moved next.

Some plurals of money, distance, and time call for a singular verb.

>Incorrect: *Three dollars are* enough to buy that.

>Correct: *Three dollars is* enough to buy that.

For words declaring degrees of quantity such as *many of, some of,* or *most of,* let the noun that follows of be the guide:

> Incorrect: *Many of the books is* in the shelf.

> Correct: *Many of the books are* in the shelf.

> Incorrect: *Most of the pie are* on the table.

> Correct: *Most of the pie is* on the table.

For indefinite pronouns like *anybody* or *everybody*, use singular verbs.

> *Everybody is* going to the store.

However, the pronouns *few, many, several, all, some,* and *both* have their own rules and use plural forms.

> Some *are* ready.

Some nouns like *crowd* and *congress* are called *collective nouns* and they require a singular verb form.

> *Congress is* in session.

> The *news is* over.

Books and movie titles, though, including plural nouns such as *Great Expectations*, also require a singular verb. Remember that only the subject affects the verb. While writing tricky subject-verb arrangements, say them aloud. Listen to them. Once the rules have been learned, one's ear will become sensitive to them, making it easier to pick out what's right and what's wrong.

Direct Objects

The **direct object** is the part of the sentence that receives the action of the verb. It is a noun and can usually be found after the verb. To find the direct object, first find the verb, and then ask the question *who* or *what* after it.

> The bear climbed the tree.

> What did the bear climb? *the tree*

Indirect Objects

An **indirect object** receives the direct object. It is usually found between the verb and the direct object. A strategy for identifying the indirect object is to find the verb and ask the questions *to whom/for whom* or *to what/for what*.

> Jane made her daughter a cake.

> For whom did Jane make the cake? *her daughter*

Cake is the direct object because it is what Jane made, and *daughter* is the indirect object because she receives the cake.

Homonyms

Homonyms are words that sound the same but are spelled differently, and they have different meanings. There are several common homonyms that give writers trouble.

There, They're, and Their

The word *there* can be used as an adverb, adjective, or pronoun:

There are ten children on the swim team this summer.

I put my book over *there*, but now I can't find it.

The word *they're* is a contraction of the words *they* and *are*:

They're flying in from Texas on Tuesday.

The word *their* is a possessive pronoun:

I store *their* winter clothes in the attic.

Its and It's

Its is a possessive pronoun:

The cat licked *its* injured paw.

It's is the contraction for the words *it* and *is*:

It's unbelievable how many people opted not to vote in the last election.

Your and You're

Your is a possessive pronoun:

Can I borrow *your* lawnmower this weekend?

You're is a contraction for the words *you* and *are*:

You're about to embark on a fantastic journey.

To, Too, and Two

To is an adverb or a preposition used to show direction, relationship, or purpose:

We are going *to* New York.

They are going *to* see a show.

Too is an adverb that means more than enough, also, and very:

> You have had *too* much candy.

> We are on vacation that week, *too*.

Two is the written-out form of the numeral 2:

> *Two* of the shirts didn't fit, so I will have to return them.

New and Knew

New is an adjective that means recent:

> There's a *new* customer on the phone.

Knew is the past tense of the verb *know*:

> I *knew* you'd have fun on this ride.

Affect and Effect

Affect and *effect* are complicated because they are used as both nouns and verbs, have similar meanings, and are pronounced the same.

	Affect	**Effect**
Noun Definition	emotional state	result
Noun Example	The patient's affect was flat.	The effects of smoking are well documented.
Verb Definition	to influence	to bring about
Verb Example	The pollen count affects my allergies.	The new candidate hopes to effect change.

Independent and Dependent Clauses

Independent clauses and **dependent clauses** are strings of words that contain both a subject and a verb. An independent clause *can* stand alone as a complete thought, but a dependent clause *cannot*. A dependent clause relies on other words to be a complete sentence.

> Independent clause: The keys are on the counter.

> Dependent clause: If the keys are on the counter

Notice that both clauses have a subject (*keys*) and a verb (*are*). The independent clause expresses a complete thought, but the word *if* at the beginning of the dependent clause makes it *dependent* on other words to be a complete thought.

> Independent clause: If the keys are on the counter, please give them to me.

This presents a complete sentence since it includes at least one verb and one subject and is a complete thought. In this case, the independent clause has two subjects (*keys* & an implied *you*) and two verbs (*are* & *give*).

Independent clause: I went to the store.

Dependent clause: Because we are out of milk,

Complete Sentence: Because we are out of milk, I went to the store.

Complete Sentence: I went to the store because we are out of milk.

Phrases

A **phrase** is a group of words that do not make a complete thought or a clause. They are parts of sentences or clauses. Phrases can be used as nouns, adjectives, or adverbs. A phrase does not contain both a subject and a verb.

Prepositional Phrases

A **prepositional phrase** shows the relationship between a word in the sentence and the object of the preposition. The object of the preposition is a noun that follows the preposition.

The orange pillows are on the couch.

On is the preposition, and *couch* is the object of the preposition.

She brought her friend with the nice car.

With is the preposition, and *car* is the object of the preposition. Here are some common prepositions:

about	as	at	after
by	for	from	in
of	on	to	with

Verbals and Verbal Phrases

Verbals are forms of verbs that act as other parts of speech. They can be used as nouns, adjectives, or adverbs. Though they use verb forms, they are not to be used as the verb in the sentence. A word group that is based on a verbal is considered a **verbal phrase**. There are three major types of verbals: participles, gerunds, and infinitives.

Participles are verbals that act as adjectives. The present participle ends in *–ing*, and the past participle ends in *–d, -ed, -n,* or *-t.*

Verb	Present Participle	Past Participle
walk	walking	walked
share	sharing	shared

Participial phrases are made up of the participle and modifiers, complements, or objects.

Crying for most of an hour, the baby didn't seem to want to nap.

Having already taken this course, the student was bored during class.

Crying for most of an hour and *Having already taken this course* are the participial phrases.

Gerunds are verbals that are used as nouns and end in *–ing*. A gerund can be the subject or object of the sentence like a noun. Note that a present participle can also end in *–ing*, so it is important to distinguish between the two. The gerund is used as a noun, while the participle is used as an adjective.

Swimming is my favorite sport.

I wish I were *sleeping*.

A **gerund phrase** includes the gerund and any modifiers or complements, direct objects, indirect objects, or pronouns.

Cleaning the house is my least favorite weekend activity.

Cleaning the house is the gerund phrase acting as the subject of the sentence.

The most important goal this year is raising money for charity.

Raising money for charity is the gerund phrase acting as the direct object.

An **infinitive** is a verbal made up of the word to and a verb. Infinitives can be used as nouns, adjectives, or adverbs.

Examples: *To eat, to jump, to swim, to lie, to call, to work*

An **infinitive phrase** is made up of the infinitive plus any complements or modifiers. The infinitive phrase *to wait* is used as the subject in this sentence:

To wait was not what I had in mind.

The infinitive phrase *to sing* is used as the subject complement in this sentence:

Her dream is to sing.

The infinitive phrase *to grow* is used as an adverb in this sentence:

Children must eat to grow.

Four Types of Sentence Structures

A **simple sentence** has one independent clause.

I am going to win.

A **compound sentence** has two independent clauses. A conjunction—*for, and, nor, but, or, yet, so*—links them together. Note that each of the independent clauses has a subject and a verb.

I am going to win, but the odds are against me.

A **complex sentence** has one independent clause and one or more dependent clauses.

I am going to win, even though I don't deserve it.

Even though I don't deserve it is a dependent clause. It does not stand on its own. Some conjunctions that link an independent and a dependent clause are *although*, *because*, *before*, *after*, *that*, *when*, *which*, and *while*.

A **compound-complex sentence** has at least three clauses, two of which are independent and at least one that is a dependent clause.

While trying to dance, I tripped over my partner's feet, but I regained my balance quickly.

The dependent clause is *While trying to dance*.

Sentence Fragments

A **sentence fragment** is an incomplete sentence. An independent clause is made up of a subject and a predicate, and both are needed to make a complete sentence.

Sentence fragments often begin with relative pronouns (*when, which*), subordinating conjunctions (*because, although*) or gerunds (*trying, being, seeing*). They might be missing the subject or the predicate.

The most common type of fragment is the isolated dependent clause, which can be corrected by joining it to the independent clause that appears before or after the fragment:

Fragment: While the cookies baked.

Correction: While the cookies baked, we played cards.

Run-On Sentences

A **run-on sentence** is created when two independent clauses are joined without correct punctuation or a conjunction. Run-on sentences can be corrected in the following ways:

- Join the independent clauses with a comma and coordinating conjunction.

    Run-on: We forgot to return the library books we had to pay a fine.

    Correction: We forgot to return the library books, so we had to pay a fine.

- Join the independent clauses with a semicolon, dash, or colon when the clauses are closely related in meaning.

    Run-on: I had a salad for lunch every day this week I feel healthier already.

    Correction: I had a salad for lunch every day this week; I feel healthier already.

- Join the independent clauses with a semicolon and a conjunctive adverb.

  Run-on: We arrived at the animal shelter on time however the dog had already been adopted.

  Correction: We arrived at the animal shelter on time; however, the dog had already been adopted.

- Separate the independent clauses into two sentences with a period.

  Run-on: He tapes his favorite television show he never misses an episode.

  Correction: He tapes his favorite television show. He never misses an episode.

- *Rearrange the wording* of the sentence to create an independent clause and a dependent clause.

  Run-on: My wedding date is coming up I am getting more excited to walk down the aisle.

  Correction: As my wedding date approaches, I am getting more excited to walk down the aisle.

Dangling and Misplaced Modifiers

A **modifier** is a phrase that describes, alters, limits, or gives more information about a word in the sentence. The two most common issues are dangling and misplaced modifiers.

A **dangling modifier** is created when the phrase modifies a word that is not clearly stated in the sentence.

  Dangling modifier: Having finished dinner, the dishes were cleared from the table.

  Correction: Having finished dinner, Amy cleared the dishes from the table.

In the first sentence, *having finished dinner* appears to modify *the dishes*, which obviously can't finish dinner. The second sentence adds the subject *Amy*, to make it clear who has finished dinner.

  Dangling modifier: Hoping to improve test scores, all new books were ordered for the school.

  Correction: Hoping to improve test scores, administrators ordered all new books for the school.

Without the subject *administrators*, it appears the books are hoping to improve test scores, which doesn't make sense.

Misplaced modifiers are placed incorrectly in the sentence, which can cause confusion. Compare these examples:

  Misplaced modifier: Rory purchased a new flat screen television and placed it on the wall above the fireplace, with all the bells and whistles.

  Revised: Rory purchased a new flat screen television, with all the bells and whistles, and placed it on the wall above the fireplace.

The bells and whistles should modify the television, not the fireplace. Let's look at another example.

Misplaced modifier: The delivery driver arrived late with the pizza, who was usually on time.

Revised: The delivery driver, who usually was on time, arrived late with the pizza.

This suggests that the delivery driver was usually on time, instead of the pizza.

Misplaced modifier: We saw a family of ducks on the way to church.

Revised: On the way to church, we saw a family of ducks.

The misplaced modifier suggests the *ducks* were on their way to church, instead of the pronoun *we*.

Double Negatives

A **double negative** is a negative statement that includes two negative elements. This is incorrect in Standard English.

Incorrect: She hasn't never come to my house to visit.

Correct: She has never come to my house to visit.

The intended meaning is that she has never come to the house, so the double negative is incorrect. However, it is possible to use two negatives to create a positive statement.

Correct: She was not unhappy with her performance on the quiz.

In this case, the double negative, *was not unhappy*, is intended to show a positive, so it is correct. This means that she was somewhat happy with her performance.

Faulty Parallelism

It is necessary to use parallel construction in sentences that have multiple similar ideas. Using parallel structure provides clarity in writing. **Faulty parallelism** is created when multiple ideas are joined using different sentence structures. Compare these examples:

Incorrect: We start each practice with stretches, a run, and fielding grounders.

Correct: We start each practice with stretching, running, and fielding grounders.

Incorrect: I watched some television, reading my book, and fell asleep.

Correct: I watched some television, read my book, and fell asleep.

Subjects Joined by Or and Nor

Compound subjects joined by *or* or *nor* rely on the subject nearest to the verb to determine conjugation and agreement:

Neither Ben nor Jeff was in attendance at the conference.

Pink or purple is the bride's color choice.

In each example, the subjects are both singular, so the verb should be singular.

If one subject is singular and the other plural, the subject nearest to the verb is the one that needs to agree:

Either the shirt or pants are hanging on the clothesline.

In this example, there is a singular subject (*shirt*) and a plural subject (*pants*), so the verb (*are*) should agree with the subject nearest to it (*pants*).

Practice Questions

[1]I have to admit that when my father bought an RV, I thought he was making a huge mistake. [2]In fact, I even thought he might have gone a little bit crazy. [3]I did not really know anything about recreational vehicles, but I knew that my dad was as big a "city slicker" as there was. [4]On trips to the beach, he preferred to swim at the pool, and whenever he went hiking, he avoided touching any plants for fear that they might be poison ivy. [5]Why would this man, with an almost irrational fear of the outdoors, want a 40-foot camping behemoth?

[6]The RV was a great purchase for our family and brought us all closer together. [7]Every morning we would wake up, eat breakfast, and broke camp. [8]We laughed at our own comical attempts to back The Beast into spaces that seemed impossibly small. [9]We rejoiced when we figured out how to "hack" a solution to a nagging technological problem. [10]When things inevitably went wrong and we couldn't solve the problems on our own, we discovered the incredible helpfulness and friendliness of the RV community. We even made some new friends in the process.

[11] Above all, owning the RV allowed us to share adventures travelling across America that we could not have experienced in cars and hotels. [12]Enjoying a campfire on a chilly summer evening with the mountains of Glacier National Park in the background, or waking up early in the morning to see the sun rising over the distant spires of Arches National Park are memories that will always stay with me and our entire family. [13]Those are also memories that my siblings and I have now shared with our own children.

1. How should the author change sentence 11?
    a. Above all, it will allow us to share adventures travelling across America that we could not have experienced in cars and hotels.
    b. Above all, it allows you to share adventures travelling across America that you could not have experienced in cars and hotels.
    c. Above all, it allowed us to share adventures travelling across America that we could not have experienced in cars and hotels.
    d. Above all, it allows them to share adventures travelling across America that they could not have experienced in cars and hotels.

2. Which of the following examples would make a good addition to the selection after sentence 4?
    a. My father is also afraid of seeing insects.
    b. My father is surprisingly good at starting a campfire.
    c. My father negotiated contracts for a living.
    d. My father isn't even bothered by pigeons.

3. Which of the following would correct the error in sentence 7?
    a. Every morning we would wake up, ate breakfast, and broke camp.
    b. Every morning we would wake up, eat breakfast, and broke camp.
    c. Every morning we would wake up, eat breakfast, and break camp.
    d. Every morning we would wake up, ate breakfast, and break camp.

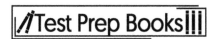

4. What transition word could be added to the beginning of sentence 6?
    a. Not surprisingly,
    b. Furthermore,
    c. As it turns out,
    d. Of course,

5. Which of the following topics would fit well between paragraph 1 and paragraph 2?
    a. A guide to RV holding tanks
    b. Describing how RV travel is actually not as outdoors-oriented as many think
    c. A description of different types of RVs
    d. Some examples of how other RV enthusiasts helped the narrator and his father during their travels

Answer Explanations

1. C: The sentence should be in the same tense and person as the rest of the selection. The rest of the selection is in past tense and first person. Choice *A* is in future tense. Choice *B* is in second person. Choice *D* is in third person. While none of these sentences are incorrect by themselves, they are written in a tense that is different from the rest of the selection. Only Choice *C* maintains tense and voice consistent with the rest of the selection.

2. A: Choices *B* and *D* go against the point the author is trying to make—that the father is not comfortable in nature. Choice *C* is irrelevant to the topic. Choice *A* is the only choice that emphasizes the father's discomfort with spending time in nature.

3. C: This sentence uses verbs in a parallel series, so each verb must follow the same pattern. In order to fit with the helping verb "would," each verb must be in the present tense. In Choices *A*, *B*, and *D*, one or more of the verbs switches to past tense. Only Choice *C* remains in the same tense, maintaining the pattern.

4. C: In paragraph 2, the author surprises the reader by asserting that the opposite of what was expected was in fact true—the city slicker father actually enjoyed the RV experience. Only Choice *C* indicates this shift in expected outcome, while the other choices indicate a continuation of the previous expectation.

5. B: Choices *A* and *C* are irrelevant to the topic. They deal more with details about RVs while the author is more concerned with the family's experiences with them. Choice *D* is relevant to the topic, but it would fit better between paragraphs 2 and 3, since the author does not mention this point until the end of the second paragraph. Choice *B* would help explain to the reader why the father, who does not enjoy the outdoors, could end up enjoying RVs so much.

Verbal Expression

Identifying the Clearest and Most Accurate Report of an Incident

Incidents can happen so quickly it can be hard to process the information immediately in a clear and accurate way. Many reports of incidents a police officer will come across will have the same scattered train of thought and may often be difficult to decipher. Spotting the clearest report of an incident means being able to interpret and reorganize data into more coherent forms to make the facts simpler to recognize. To spot clear information, it is important to look out for concise wording, clear phrasing, and a logical progression of events. Concise wording gives emphasis to the facts presented in the report; words are straightforward and do not ramble. Clear phrasing of an incident presents the information in a way that can be easily understood and not require unnecessary interpretation. The clearest report will have consistent grammar with sentences that make sense to the listener or reader. The information will be easily read out loud without further clarifications. Also, a report with a logical progression of events presents the information with a clear beginning, middle, and end so the reader can easily understand how an incident occurred from the observer's perspective.

However, just because information is presented clearly does not necessarily make it accurate. Identifying accurate information means recognizing what is the most important, factual evidence in a report. An accurate report is unambiguous and makes logical sense when compared with the incident as a whole. Spotting accurate information also requires a police officer to recognize which information sounds the most credible when presented with multiple accounts. A credible source will present the event completely, without conflicting ideas or opinions. Useful sources will give their full perspective, sticking to their story, without judgments or misleading evidence that may not relate to the incident. The most accurate report is the one that remains the most objective, relaying events exactly as they occurred and emphasizing clarity. By identifying the clearest and most accurate report, the police officer is organizing the details needed to develop a case.

Writing Clear Case Reports

After gathering the appropriate information, it is time to write the case report of an incident. In order for others to get a clear and accurate picture of what took place, it is important for the case report to be written in a manner that can be easily understood and interpreted. The facts need to be established and presented in a way that can be read by anyone, giving them a full understanding of the incident as a whole, as reported by the police officer. Writing a clear case report requires proper grammar and logic, a thorough presentation and explanation of the objective facts, and a professional, well-developed opinion based on the facts.

Using proper grammar will ensure that writing is clear and makes sense. Sentence structure rules should be followed in order for others to be able to clearly understand the report. The logic of the information should also progress in a way that is easy to comprehend. An officer should start with what happened first and then draw conclusions based on the progression of events. An officer also has to ensure they have written all the facts they are aware of in the case and be able to interpret the data they are given in order to identify the facts relating to the incident. Each fact should directly relate to the occasion and be free of any outside opinion. A clear case report depends on the facts to explain what occurred; if the facts are misplaced or untrue, there can be no clear picture of what happened. After all the facts have been laid out and identified, it is then the officer's job to interpret the facts and form their own opinions on how and why the incident occurred. A complete case report includes clear, understandable information, all the facts, and additional insights of the reporting officer to further express the case in a way that others can expand upon to help solve it.

Drawing Logical Conclusions Related to Police Scenarios

Many situations will require the reporting officer to make logical conclusions based on data acquired relating to an incident. Information will need to be interpreted in order for the correct actions to be taken. Actions such as the best time to patrol an area or what to look out for to determine the best procedure can be determined by drawing logical conclusions. Some tips to keep in mind to figure out the most helpful solutions are to identify the facts, then interpret the data, and finally, identify patterns to draw relations between events.

Logical conclusions are important for making accurate judgments that will best solve a case. A careful examination of data is required to essentially determine what it all means. An officer will need to identify what information will be useful in a given scenario so they can make the most informed decision. Often, misleading evidence can set an officer on the wrong course. When making logical decisions, it is important for the officer to be completely sure by backing up their conclusions with evidence and to only make final decisions when they are absolutely sure all the data is conclusive and the actions will lead to a solution.

The logical conclusion is one that brings together related details to problem-solve. The first step to **drawing logical conclusions** is to identify all the facts of a case. The next step is to look at all the facts to start interpreting the data. Once all the facts have been identified, the details that are the most relevant to the situation can be determined; these will be the key points to use when drawing conclusions. The next step is to look for a pattern in the information, use these patterns to progress the information to a logical end, and interpret what may happen next or what may have happened before the incident based on the progression of the facts. It is important to look for gaps in the information and fill them in with what may have occurred or what might need to occur for the data to be the most useful. Finally, conclusions based on how the information has been interpreted and progressed should be made. The final conclusion should include the recommended action to best use the data and solve the incident.

Reading a Set of Laws and an Action Taken by an Officer and Determining Whether the Officer Acted Correctly

In addition to interpreting data from a report, a police officer will be expected to examine the interpretations and conclusions of other officers to determine whether the correct actions were taken or what went wrong in a given incident. Cross-checking between different officers is important to ensure accuracy and to evaluate the proper actions to take regarding a specific incident. To determine the correct action to take, the officer must first examine and understand the laws that relate to the incident. Once this has been done, they can determine the corresponding action to take according to the law. This action can then be compared to the action taken by another officer to determine its correctness.

An officer will need to use their own, educated judgment when determining how correct another officer's actions are because not all solutions will be explicitly spelled out in the law books or research. An officer must be able to place themselves within the situation to determine what they would have done differently and what the results of those actions would be. The officer must also determine why the actions of the other officer were correct or not. An incorrect action will often result in more problems and further reports, whereas a correct action settles the problem better and can be clearly understood. Actions that are ambiguous or seem to not follow the logical pattern suggested by the

interpretation of the law would be considered incorrect. If an officer acted incorrectly, an example of what actions should be taken to remedy any problems in addition to what exactly the officer did incorrectly should be considered. Any discrepancy between the law and the officer's actions should then be reported.

Understanding Provided Legal Definitions and Applying Them to Typical Police Situations

It is important for a police officer to have a thorough understanding of provided legal definitions. An officer needs to completely understand what laws a certain situation involves so they can determine the correct action to take based on those legal definitions. The completely correct action may often be hard to determine because right and wrong can be difficult to objectively define. The best way to determine the correct course of action is to interpret each situation in relation to the legal definition that relates to similar instances. An incorrect action would not necessarily be what is subjectively morally correct but the one that makes the most sense in relation to the way the government has legally defined the situation to progress in order to avoid disputes of opinion.

To understand a provided legal definition, the officer needs to be able to apply what is written to real-world examples. Definitions are by nature very general in order to include as many scenarios as possible, so the officer needs to determine why their individual scenario will fit the definition. An officer should look for key words used in reports to determine what definition to use as well as look for what law is being broken. Often, more than one definition will be needed because incidents will involve more than one specific legal specification. It is important to start with the most general crime or case involved and then get more technical by including detailed information and determining how the incident is related to any subsidiaries of the definition.

To apply the legal definition to the specific case, it will be necessary to identify why the legal definition fits. This can be accomplished by looking at the nature of the incident: Is it a theft? Is someone injured? Is there a domestic dispute? Can the situation be easily solved by the definition chosen, or is there more to the situation? An officer may need to use logical experimentation to determine if a definition fits the incident and mentally play out the suggested actions of several legal definitions to determine which would work best for the given situation. A definition that works is one that identifies the possible crimes committed and provides the best plan of action to take as determined by similar instances in the past. If the definition only covers part of the crimes that took place, an officer should continue finding definitions until the entire scope of the situation has been interpreted and definitions have been found for each term used to describe what took place.

Reading a Report About a Crime in a Certain Area, With Times Crimes Were Committed, and Selecting the Best Time to Patrol the Area

To make the best use of patrol time, an officer will need to read and interpret crime reports for their assigned patrol area. Reports about crime in a certain area provide statistical data and location details for the crimes. The general location will be listed and recorded as neighborhood blocks, landmarks, or strips of road. The day of the week along with the most prevalent times that crimes are reported will also be detailed. The data is often broken down and represented as averages; this way, an officer can read when specific crimes are most likely to occur based on what has been reported the most in the past. The officer can then determine when and what area to patrol to deter a certain type of crime from occurring. Reports about crime in the area are useful to establish how to best allocate time by setting aside a specific objective or crime to target.

To select the best time to patrol a given area, an officer must first look to find the section of the report that gives the details about the specific crime they want to deter. A lot of information will be contained in these reports, so it will be important to choose only the specific, key information that can be used to determine the best area to patrol. Finding and combining the day, time, and place a crime has been reported the most will give the officer the information needed to decide when and where to patrol. The place and time when the incidents of a specific crime are reported are the areas where they are most likely to occur again, giving the officer the best chance of finding and stopping another occurrence. An officer should also keep in mind that it is important to arrive approximately an hour ahead and stay an hour later than the reported times so they can be ready and on the scene to spot all possible occurrences.

Interpreting Police Information Given in Tables, Charts, and Graphs

Often, an officer may only have written data in the form of tables, charts, and/or graphs instead of sensory information as evidence to be used to make decisions. An officer will need to be able to understand how to read and interpret these forms of information to help reach more informed conclusions. This requires attention to detail and patience when searching for relevant information. Large amounts of data are collected so that officers have the most resources available; however, the growing amount of information can sometimes make it hard to find exactly what they are looking for. The better an officer understands the various ways to find and use data presented in tables, charts, and graphs, the quicker they will be able to find the data without wasting too much time with irrelevant information.

The most important and helpful information to use when interpreting data in the form of tables, charts, and graphs are the titles and labels that identify what information is being presented. On data tables, this information will usually be displayed at the very top of the table, with descriptive headings for the information listed below. The titles will also sometimes be formatted in a way that stands out from the other information (often in bold) and have general names instead of listing specific data. Tables are usually presented as grids, and to find the information needed, the officer will need to locate the specific heading and follow the grid down to the data. Charts are similar to tables, but they can encompass a larger range of visual effects, displaying information in a more creative, open way. It can be hard to determine exactly what form a chart will take, but titles and labels will often be included in separate areas called a key or legend. This area will inform the researcher on where and how the data they need is displayed. On a graph, the horizontal axis at the bottom of the graph and the vertical axis on the left side of the graph will contain the titles, representing changes in variables in relation to each other. Graphs will sometimes also contain legends or keys to further describe the data being presented. The best way for a police officer to interpret tables, charts, and graphs is to have a clear understanding of what they are looking for and what the data represents by paying close attention to the way the information is laid out.

Defining a Crime Committed With the Appropriate Statute

Statutes are laws that are written by a country's government to determine policies and prohibit behaviors or items/possessions. They are different from laws that are determined by court cases because they are passed by legislature instead of arrived at over judge rulings. Statutes are used to define the type of crime committed for use in prosecutions. Finding the appropriate statute dictates the proceedings or actions to be taken regarding an incident. It is important for an officer to be familiar with federal and state statutes when filing a case in order to determine the correct course of action to take.

Statutes cover all types of laws, not just criminal offenses. This is why it is important to know what statute will apply to what situation. When determining the appropriate statute to use, it is necessary to look for what type of general offense is being committed and ask: What makes the incident a crime? What went wrong, and who is the harmed party? The officer should read a few definitions that may fit. Which one seems like it encompasses the situation the best? Are there sub-definitions that are more specific that can apply more exclusively to the situation? It is important to start with the most general outcome of the crime and then look at the details to see if anything is missing in the chosen definition. The officer should apply multiple statutes to an instance if more than one offense was committed and look for words that match the report of the incident and think of synonyms for the words that may be more frequently used in documents with law language. An officer should be familiar with the language and jargon of the industry and how to interpret these definitions to match real-world examples. The appropriate statute will dictate what comes next in the criminal process and the solving of a case by relating the incident to legal terms that can be used to prosecute offenders.

Selecting the Most Relevant Details When Given a Report

Different situations call for different details to be examined. Sometimes a report of an incident will include information unrelated to the case. An officer needs to be able to spot and determine what the most relevant details are when examining a report in relation to the specific incident. Reports are often unorganized and may read more like trains of thought than a specific detailing of what happened. Although it is important that as many details about the case as possible should be examined, too much detail can confuse investigators and lead to incorrect conclusions.

One thing an officer can do to make sure they have all the relevant information in a report is to reorganize the information as a progression of time. The officer should start with what happened first, then next, and finally, what the outcome of the action was. Details related to the sequence of events will be the most relevant information to use when determining the facts. Information unrelated to the event can be put aside to examine later after the scope of the incident is more clearly laid out. An officer should also take note of the clearest, most specific details of a case because these have the most credibility and can be proven. An example would be specific names and places of events. When the key details of the people and places involved in the report are identified, a clearer picture of the scene can be created, and the remaining sequence of events can be better thought of and analyzed. After the case has been reorganized and read over several times to find key information, the officer will have a thorough understanding of the case and be able to determine what information should be used to help find a solution.

Determining the Best Course of Action in a Police Scenario

Officers will be required to make many important decisions on the job. To determine the best course of action to take, the officer needs to have a firm grasp of their surroundings and the details of the scenario. The best course of action will be the one that makes the most logical sense at the given time. Doing too much or too little may result in complications that will make the situation harder to assess and solve or bring more danger to those involved. In order for an officer to determine the best course of action, they need to understand the facts, their limits, and the possible outcomes of their decision.

Understanding the facts in any scenario will help to determine what actions should be taken. When an officer is able to gather data beforehand and has time to process the severity of the situation, they can make more informed decisions. The more relevant information an officer has, the better the ability they have to relate the information to similar occurrences in the past so they can decide what the best course of action will be. The facts in any case will help when reporting about the specifics of the incident and justifying actions taken. An officer also has to understand the limits of their ability when faced with police scenarios. They need to know when to ask for help or when to stay away from a situation until a more advantageous time arises. Realizing the dangers of the situation and preparing accordingly will save a lot of time and possibly lives. In certain cases, it can be helpful to do a risk and benefit analysis of each possible action to be taken to determine the safest plan. An officer should make a clear assessment in the risk analysis of the resources available and how they can best be utilized. After the situation has been assessed, it is important for the officer to hypothesize a few different decisions quickly to mentally play out how each one may affect the case. Thinking ahead of acting is very important for an officer, and no action should be taken without considering how that outcome may affect those involved. Even in the instances where a decision needs to be made immediately, an officer needs to be able to think clearly about the situation in order to justify their actions.

Practice Questions

1. OFFICER NOTES: About 2:30 a.m., December 22, 2019, I visited a house in Phoenix, AZ, at 11345 N. 32nd Drive to talk to a woman identifying herself as Laura Palmer regarding a reported domestic abuse issue.

Which of the following choices most clearly and accurately presents the facts from the report above?
   a. After I received a call in Phoenix, AZ, December 22, 2019, I visited the victim of domestic abuse, 11345 N. 32nd Drive, 2:30 a.m., Laura Palmer.
   b. When I pulled in to visit at 11345 N. 32nd Drive at 2:30 a.m. on December 22, I saw a woman in front of the house named Laura Palmer who reported a domestic abuse dispute.
   c. I responded to a call at 2:30 a.m., December 22, 2019, at 11345 N. 32nd Drive. When I arrived, I spoke to a woman who identified herself as Laura Palmer. She said she was reporting a domestic abuse issue.
   d. I responded to a domestic abuse dispute by driving to a house in Phoenix, AZ, and meeting with Laura Palmer.

2. OFFICER NOTES: I responded to a report of a vehicle accident in Phoenix, AZ, off the Loop 202 and 45th Street, at 3:00 p.m. When I arrived, there was one red pickup truck on the side of the road with a bent rear bumper. The owner of the pickup truck, identifying himself as Mark Maron, told me another driver of a white van crashed into his rear bumper and drove off.

   Which of the following presents the clearest case report using the information given above?
   a. There was a vehicular accident in Phoenix, AZ, off the Loop 202 and 45th Street, at 3:00 p.m. There will be no witnesses. If this Mark Maron is telling the truth, it would be hard to believe he is not.
   b. At 3:00 p.m., an officer responded to a vehicle accident report in Phoenix, AZ, off the Loop 202 and 45th Street. When the officer arrived, he witnessed a red pickup truck at the side of the road with its rear bumper bent. The owner of the vehicle identified himself as Mark Maron, who reported that a white van crashed into the rear of his truck and then drove off. There were no reported witnesses. However, it is my opinion that the driver is telling the truth because the dents at the back of his truck prove his statement, even though he could not completely identify the license plate number of the car that hit him. It is my recommendation that a report be filed and made available for the insurance company if requested and any white vans with bent front ends be searched for in the immediate area.
   c. 3:00 p.m. Phoenix, AZ. A red truck with a bent bumper. Mark Maron. Vehicle hit-and-run. Let's search for the culprit.
   d. It was 3:00 p.m. when a Mark Maron reported that his red pickup truck was hit by a white van that drove away. He was met by an officer off the Loop 202 and 45th Street when the call was made. The officer did not report any witnesses. It is my opinion that the culprit be searched for in the immediate area and a report be prepared just in case. There were also dents in the back of the red pickup truck.

93

3. An officer responds to a report of a domestic dispute. When the officer arrives, a man greets the officer and says nothing is wrong. A woman is sitting behind the man, hiding her face, silently crying. There are clothes and objects laying around the house in disarray.

Which of the following conclusions can be made from the statement above?
    a. There really is nothing wrong; the call was misleading.
    b. The man is being untruthful; the distressed woman and disorderly house indicate a dispute.
    c. An officer already came by and cleared up the incident.
    d. A drug deal is about to be conducted; the man is nervous and wants the officer to leave. There is also evidence the woman may be on drugs.

4. Officer Brian responded to a report of drugs being consumed in a private, commercial parking lot. When Officer Brian arrived, he searched several cars in the area where the reports came from until he found the drugs. However, the individual in possession of the drugs says they were searched unlawfully because they were not near their car during the time of the search and had not been asked beforehand if their vehicle could be inspected.

Based on the information above, which of the following is correct?
    a. Officer Brian acted correctly.
    b. Officer Brian acted incorrectly; he needed probable cause for a specific vehicle before he could search any vehicle.
    c. Officer Brian acted incorrectly; he should not have admitted he searched any vehicle until the culprit confessed.
    d. Officer Brian acted incorrectly; he needed a witness before accusing the culprit.

5. Officer Steven stopped a car that was speeding down the freeway. The license, registration, and insurance were up to date, but the officer did not like the driver's tone of voice and asked him to step out of the vehicle. The driver refused, so Officer Steven pulled him out of the vehicle, used pepper spray to subdue him, and then cuffed and arrested him. The driver reported unnecessary force and claims he did nothing wrong.

Based on the report above, which of the following is correct?
    a. Officer Steven acted correctly.
    b. Officer Steven acted incorrectly; he should have arrested the driver without force.
    c. Officer Steven acted incorrectly; he did not obtain a search warrant.
    d. Officer Steven acted incorrectly; he should not have arrested the driver or used force.

Answer Explanations

1. C: The clearest and most accurate report lists all the details given in the Officer Notes in a logical way that progresses from start to finish. Choice A jumbles some of the information regarding the time of the report by putting it in a place that does not make much sense. Choice B ignores the city and presents the information more as a coincidental experience. Choice D leaves out some vital information and lacks detail.

2. B: The clearest case report presents the information using all the officer's resources in a clear, logical order. Choice A and Choice C lack all the information, and they are presented in a way that is not completely clear. Choice D has all the relevant information and includes an opinion on what actions should take place, but the information is not presented with clear progression.

3. B: There is a bigger picture to be investigated based on drawing logical conclusions from the evidence, and further investigation would be warranted. Choice A is incorrect because even though the man says there is nothing wrong, an officer surveying the scene can detect the clues that indicate a dispute had indeed taken place. However, there is no conclusive indication another officer had already been there or that there are any drugs involved, making Choices C and D incorrect.

4. B: The law generally states that an officer needs verbal permission, an issued warrant, or probable cause before they can search someone's vehicle. Officer Brian acted incorrectly when he chose to inspect all the vehicles in the parking lot, making Choice A incorrect. Choice C and Choice D are incorrect because although they acknowledge the officer acted incorrectly, the reason for the incorrect action does not match the reading of the set of laws in this situation.

5. D: According to the law, having a disagreeable tone of voice is not grounds for arresting someone or using force when there was no threat. Therefore, Choice A and Choice B are incorrect. The law in this case does not pertain to any search warrant either, making Choice C also incorrect.

Reasoning

Law enforcement officers use their powers of observation to gather information. Through their reasoning skillsets, they'll make inferences and draw conclusions about information and evidence.

Very broadly, **reasoning** is an approach to thinking that prioritizes logic. Law enforcement officers use reasoning every day when forming judgments about suspects, piecing together timelines, and evaluating crime scenes.

There are three general types of reasoning problems:

- Comparative Values
- Numerical Series
- Similar Words

These items on the exam require searches for patterns, similarities, and relationships in order to choose the correct answer. There will be lists of statements, numbers, or words, and test takers will analyze the given information in order to answer the question.

Comparative Values

A **comparative value** item provides details about specific subjects, like types of fruit or family members, and then asks that comparisons be drawn between them. There are two possible tasks:

- Order the subjects from *least to greatest* or *greatest to least*
- Find *the value* of a certain subject

When encountering a comparative value item, it's helpful to make a list and fill it in according to information given in the prompt. Everything needed to answer this type of question correctly is in the question. Here's an example:

> A vehicle rental company stocks cars, vans, busses, and trucks. The company ranks their vehicles by popularity so that they know what to buy when expanding their business. Cars are ranked between vans and trucks. Trucks are more popular than vans. Buses are ranked lowest. Which type of vehicle is rented the most?
>
>   a. Cars
>   b. Vans
>   c. Busses
>   d. Trucks

C   V   T   B

The items being compared are the prompt's subjects. In this question, there are cars, vans, buses, and trucks. Assigning them a letter or an image, as illustrated above, is a helpful way to list them quickly. For this question, the first letter of each vehicle represents the subject: C (car), V (van), T (truck), and B (bus).

Note what the prompt actually asks. In this prompt, the goal is to find which vehicle is rented *the most*. Thus, the list needs to be ordered from *most to least*:

Vehicles Rented – Most to Least

Determine which information is stated outright, meaning it is known for sure. In this prompt, *buses are ranked the lowest,* so buses can be placed at the bottom of the list:

Vehicles Rented – Most to Least
B

Next, look through the prompt for more information. This prompt states that *cars are ranked between vans and trucks,* so the list can look one of two ways:

Vehicles Rented – Most to Least **Possibility 1**	Vehicles Rented – Most to Least **Possibility 2**
V	T
C	C
T	V
B	B

To decide which list is correct, look for the last piece of information given in the prompt. In this prompt, *trucks are more popular than vans.* Which one of the lists shows that to be true?

Vehicles Rented – Most to Least
T
C
V
B

Revisit the final question to determine the response. *Which vehicle is being rented the most?* The answer is *D*, Trucks.

Numerical Series

A **numerical series** item presents a list of numbers and asks test takers to determine what the next number should be. The key to answering this type of question correctly is to understand *the relationship between the numbers* in the series. Do they increase or decrease, and at what rate? Is there a pattern? Here's an example:

> Identify the next number in the series: 7, 14, 21, 28, 35, ...
>   a. 42
>   b. 28
>   c. 47
>   d. 50

First, decide if the numbers in the list are *increasing* or *decreasing*. Generally, if numbers increase, it is indicative of addition or multiplication. If they decrease, subtraction or division is more likely.

The numbers in this list are *increasing*: 7, 14, 21, 28, 35.

Here's a strategy to determine *the rate* at which they are increasing:

7,   14,   21,   28,   35

+7   +7   +7   +7

The numbers in the list are increasing by 7. The rate of increase is constant throughout the list. Note that not all lists will increase or decrease at a constant rate.

To find the answer to this question, simply continue the rate of increase by adding 7 to 35. The answer is *A*, 42.

Here's a more complicated example:

> Identify the next number in the series: 2, 3, 5, 9, 17...
>   a. 24
>   b. 33
>   c. 37
>   d. 39

Again, the first thing to do is decide if the numbers in the list are increasing or decreasing. The numbers in this list are *increasing*: 2, 3, 5, 9, 17.

Next, figure out the rate of increase:

2,   3,   5,   9,   17

+1   +2   +4   +8

Notice that, in this question, the rate of increase is not constant. The question needs to be solved by looking for a pattern in the rate of increase.

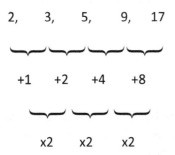

1, 2, 4, and 8 are all *multiples of 2*: $1 \times 2 = 2, 2 \times 2 = 4, 4 \times 2 = 8$. What is needed to continue this pattern? 8×2.

Given that $8 \times 2 = 16$, 16 is the next number in the rate of increase.

2,   3,   5,   9,   17

+1   +2   +4   +8   +16

x2   x2   x2   x2

So, 16 must be added to the last number in the list to find the answer: $17 + 16 = 33$. The answer is *B*, 33.

Similar Words

In **similar words** questions, there will be a set of four words. Three of the words will be similar, and one will be different. The goal is to choose the one word that is *unlike* the other three.

The key to answering these questions correctly is to e*stablish the relationship between the three similar words.* The word that does not share that relationship with the others will be the answer. Here's an example:

Three of the following words are similar, while one is different. Select the word that is different.
a. Pants
b. Closet
c. Dresses
d. Skirts

First, consider what the theme of the words is. The theme of this list seems to be *clothing.* Next, start with Choice *A* and consider how this word relates to Choice *B*. Pants can *be kept* in a closet.

In Choices *C* and *D*, dresses and skirts, like pants, can also be kept in a closet. So, three out of four of the words are articles of clothing that can be kept in a closet, rendering *closet* the word that is unlike the others. The answer is *B*, Closet.

Here's another example:

Three of the following words are similar, while one is different. Select the word that is different.

- a. Book
- b. Magazine
- c. Newspaper
- d. Reading

In this question, the theme is *reading*, which is also one of the answer choices. Choices *A*, *B*, and *C* are things that can be read. Though Choice *D*, reading, does relate to the other answer choices, it does not relate in the same way. Reading is a verb, not an object that can be read, so the word that does not belong is *D*, Reading.

Practice Questions

Directions: Officers often face situations in which they need to determine how different pieces of information relate to one another. In this section, you will be presented with information, such as a group or ordered series of facts, numbers, letters, or words. Your task is to study the various pieces of information and try to understand how they relate to one another. Mark the letter that identifies your choice on your answer sheet.

1. Three of the following words are similar, while one is different. Which one is different?
   a. Student
   b. Teacher
   c. Desk
   d. Principal

2. The families who live on Gardenia Drive keep dogs, cats, and rabbits as pets. There are 3 more cats than dogs. There are 5 more dogs than rabbits. There are 2 rabbits. How many cats live on Gardenia Drive?
   a. 10
   b. 4
   c. 2
   d. 11

3. Which of the following is the next number in the series: 2, 13, 4, 14, 8, 15...?
   a. 16
   b. 17
   c. 32
   d. 14

4. A local librarian conducts a poll to gauge what types of baked goods should be sold at the library fundraiser. Cookies are ranked between cakes and pies. Pies are ranked higher than cakes. Cream puffs receive the least number of votes. Which type of baked goods receives the most votes?
   a. Cookies
   b. Cakes
   c. Pies
   d. Cream puffs

5. Three of the following words are similar, while one is different. Which one is different?
   a. Roof
   b. Skylight
   c. Ceiling
   d. Floor

Answer Explanations

1. C: The word *desk* is not like the other three. A student, teacher, and principal are all people who are found in a school setting. A desk is an inanimate object that can be found in a school setting, rendering it different from the other three words.

2. A: The correct answer is 10. According to the prompt, there are 2 rabbits on Gardenia Drive. If there are 5 more dogs than rabbits, then there are 7 dogs. If there are 3 more cats than dogs, then 10 cats live on Gardenia Drive.

3. A: The next number in the series is 16. In this series, two patterns of increase can be found. Every other number either doubles or increases by one. So, to find the next number in the series, decide which pattern the missing number should continue. Because 2×2 is 4 and 4×2 is 8, the missing number is 16, because 8×2 is 16.

4. C: The correct answer is pies. According to the prompt, cookies are ranked between cakes and pies, and pies are ranked higher than cakes. At this point, the list should read *pies, cookies,* and *cakes*. The last information in the prompt is that cream puffs received the least number of votes, so *pies* remains at the top of the list, having the most votes received.

5. D: The word *floor* is not like the other three. A roof, skylight, and ceiling are all elements of a house or building positioned *above*. The floor is positioned *below*, making it unlike the other three words.

Spatial Orientation, Visualization, and Memorization

Reading Maps to Find the Quickest Route

An officer should be familiar with different types of visual maps so they can always know the quickest route to a specific location. Road maps, subway maps, traffic maps, bus routes, etc., should all be able to be read quickly regardless of the map's visual style. An officer will need to know how to use both online and physical maps and be able to direct themselves as well as others as to the best route to take at a given time.

Generally, the easiest way to interpret a map is to look for the map key. The key will contain all the information relating to what each symbol on the map means as well as the distance scale that determines how far areas are from each other. Some maps may have this information explained in text instead of in a separate key, so the officer will need to know where to find the information that explains how the map is to be used. Finding the quickest route then means knowing where the initial starting point is, analyzing the routes on the map, and identifying which route provides the shortest amount of travel time. It is important to remember that sometimes the shortest distance between two points is not the quickest route. Traffic patterns, stops, speed limits, or other restrictions could add more travel time depending on the route and should be taken into consideration when searching for the most efficient route.

Interpreting Visual Depictions of Traffic Incidents

In cases in which traffic patterns are involved, it is important for an officer to be able to identify where traffic incidents have occurred. Different visual representations may be used online and physically to depict these situations. An officer needs to be able to interpret this data in its different forms in order to decide where the event occurred and the best course of action to take.

It is important to look for descriptions that detail how the visual data is represented for a given traffic incident depiction. The officer should look for areas of the depiction where symbols are described or defined as well as instructional text that may detail how the information is to be interpreted. Then, once the layout of the data is clear to the officer, the visual depiction can be scanned to locate the traffic incident and the surrounding area. Different visual depictions may need to be used to identify a specific problem. In this case, the officer should look for the information that relates to the incident and gather all the data needed to completely understand the situation and be up to date on any recent changes in traffic patterns.

Memorizing Elements of Street Scenes and Answering Questions When the Image is Taken Away

The Memory section of the Police Officer Exam assesses a candidate's observational skills and his or her ability to recall facts and information. This is a very important skill that police officers must employ daily during routine job duties. For example, they are regularly required to observe prison inmates and gather information pertaining to the behavior they witnessed that they must recall at a later point in time.

On the exam, this section is typically composed of a couple of drawings or photographs that are followed by a series of multiple-choice questions. The questions are not viewable until the image is removed. Test takers examine each graphic one at a time, for approximately one to five minutes (depending on the state administering the test as well as the complexity of the image) and then the image is removed. During the observation period, it is recommended that test takers study the image as carefully as possible, first examining the overall scene and then studying it more closely to identify and memorize details. The questions that follow pertain to details from the graphic and must be completed from memory. Access to review the image again is not permitted. Because the questions pertaining to the image may address the picture on a general level as well as specific details, both elements need to be examined. For example, test takers may encounter an image of a prison cell containing several inmates who are fighting. One question may address the image as a whole, such as: "*what is the general mood of the image?*" Answer choices may be options such as *triumphant, hopeful, agitated*, and *peaceful.* In this case, *agitated* is the best choice. The majority of the questions will be about more specific details from the image. For example, questions for this same image may ask how many inmates were present in the scene, what time was displayed on the wall clock, what was the position of the cell door, or how many bars were running vertically on the window.

There are a variety of strategies that candidates employ to improve their scores in this section. Most test takers start by examining the entire image for a few seconds and then moving from this broad view to an increasingly specific study. Some people find that it works best to examine the picture in quadrants or in designated sections individually in a predetermined order to ensure that the entire image is studied without leaving gaps. Other candidates employ a variety of strategies depending on the particular image. For example, they may study the people first and then the environment surrounding the scene for an outdoor picture or start by looking at the walls and then the middle of the room indoors. Other test takers start by trying to identify context clues from the scene, such as the sun position or weather in outdoor scenes or the clock time indoors to determine the season or time of day. Then, they may move on to try to count specific figures or subjects in the scene and identify distinguishing characteristics between such figures. For example, are there a different number of males and females present? Is someone wearing a distinguishing piece of clothing such as a hat? Exam questions often address things such as the time, place, and setting of the graphic. Others ask test takers to recall the number of certain items present, or to answer questions about a specific item in the image, which can be better answered if distinguishing features of the items are noted during the study period.

It is recommended that test takers practice with a variety of images and strategies to familiarize themselves with the process and to identify those methods that work best. A sample graphic similar to those that may be encountered on the exam is provided below. Test takers should study the graphic for two minutes and then completely remove it from their view while attempting the practice questions. Test takers can practice this section an unlimited number of times with the help of a partner or friend. The partner can find any type of image and generate a few questions about it and then pass it to the test candidate to attempt.

Recognizing and Identifying Facial Features and Then Matching Sketches Among Groups of Faces

Being an officer requires keen observational skills and careful attention to detail to identify and interpret important information when it comes to solving a case. In the instance of identifying potential culprits, the officer will need to pay close attention to the features of individuals who may be involved in the incident. Sketch artists help officers by rendering images of suspects based on spoken, visual descriptions. They will then create a sketch of what the person potentially looks like, making sure the sketch is as accurate as possible so that it is identifiable to others. However, an officer will often still have to look through numerous sketches to identify a specific person. To be able to accomplish this task

and pick the most accurate drawing, the officer needs to have a strong memory of the individual particulars that make up the person they are matching with the sketch.

When identifying facial features, an officer should focus on specific details that stand out. Things that may appear more pronounced in the individual than on other faces should be taken note of as well as body modifications such as tattoos and piercings. These will help distinguish the individual from others when asked to identify them later on. However, trying to keep track of too much information may be confusing when it comes time to recall a specific face; therefore, to be sure their memory is correct, an officer should focus on the details that are the easiest to remember. They should also keep in mind that drawings will never be exact and they are searching only for the closest similarity, not the one that perfectly matches the face remembered. If an officer is having trouble recalling features or is stuck between similar options, the best choice will be the one with the most specific remembered features to match any verbal descriptions that may have been used to describe the individual to the artist.

Visualizing and Identifying Patterns and Objects

To compile the most resources available to an officer for solving cases, large amounts of data need to be collected and recorded. It will be the officer's job to interpret this data to reach accurate conclusions, turning scattered information into a more coherent case that can be visualized and interpreted. A lot of sensory data will need to be kept track of and deciphered to give the most objective description of an incident. Visual data will need to be recalled in order for situations to be recreated and utilized. The best way to organize this visual data when recalling an incident is to identify patterns and specific objects. Important information in a case will often be repeated in different ways by different people. Identifying correlating data will help determine the veracity of the information because it can be confirmed by multiple sources and noted as patterns. For example, multiple witnesses may give different information about how tall a suspect may be but each mention that the suspect had a more noticeable trait such as long hair. Another example is if each party involved agrees to the time of a car accident. When the officer starts gaining additional information and identifying more patterns that are important objects involved in a case, they can better visualize the instance to help determine the best course of action to take. Visualizations of events help an officer organize and structure an incident to examine all possible conclusions.

Recalling Information From Sets of Six Wanted Posters, Such as Details on the Wanted Person and Information About the Crimes Committed

Wanted posters are used to relay information about individuals involved in open cases. It is important for an officer to familiarize themselves with different types of wanted posters so they can identify important information that may need to be recalled later to solve a case. The more information the officer is able to take mental note of, the better equipped they will be to find and identify a wanted person. It is unreasonable to assume that all the information written on a wanted poster will be memorized by an officer, especially if multiple wanted posters are involved; however, an officer is expected to know enough about the case to recall the key details needed when the wanted poster is not available.

To know what information is the most significant to focus on, it is first important to identify how the information on the wanted poster is laid out. Most people may think of the Old West when they think about wanted posters, with bold letters identifying the criminal and the crimes committed as well as a large picture of the wanted person in the center. Wanted posters as they appear now are actually relatively unchanged from what they used to be, formatted in the same way to convey the most important information as quickly as possible. First, the officer should study the face of the individual on the poster enough to be able to recall it and then take note of the specific information, such as height, weight, and eye color, to be able to form and visualize an image of the way the complete person may appear. Once the officer is able to form a mental picture of the culprit based on the image and the description, they can then focus on the specific crimes committed in order to relate the facts of the case; these can usually be found in a text-based description surrounding the photo. Once a few of the most specific details are memorized, the officer can go to the next wanted poster and repeat the process until they can recall each individual in their mind without referring to the posters.

Practice Questions

Directions for Questions 1-5:

Examine the image below for two minutes then remove it from view. Answer the questions that follow the image without referring back to the image. Do not read the questions during the image review period.

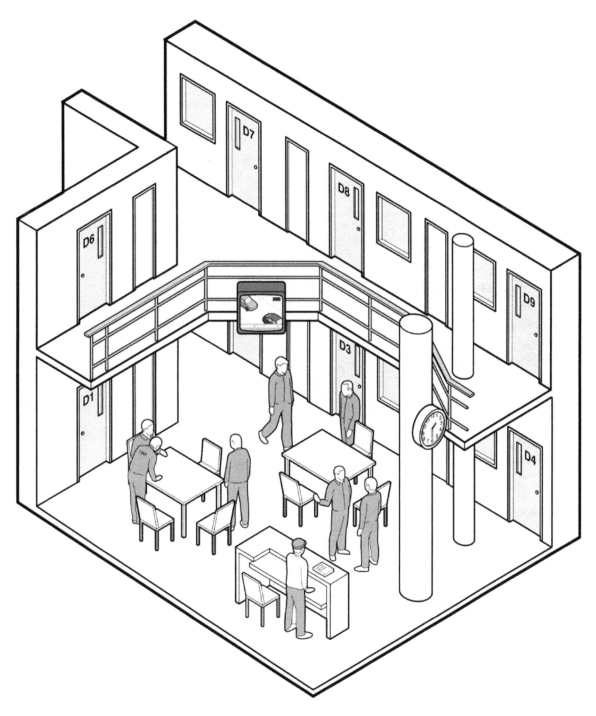

1. How many doors are located on the second floor?
    a. 1
    b. 2
    c. 3
    d. 4

2. How many inmates are located at the table on the left?
    a. 3
    b. 4
    c. 5
    d. 6

3. What time is it?
    a. 7:50
    b. 2:30
    c. 12:10
    d. 4:00

4. What is written on the right most door downstairs?
    a. D4
    b. D9
    c. C9
    d. C4

5. What was on the television?
    a. Animals
    b. A cartoon
    c. Cars
    d. The news

Answer Explanations

1. D

2. A

3. B

4. A

5. C

Information Management, Problem Sensitivity, and Situational Judgement

Ordering and Managing Facts Logically

Details for a case can build up quickly as new information comes in from different sources. Multiple people will also usually be involved in a case, making it important for an officer to be able to order and manage the facts from multiple accounts of an incident to reach the most informed conclusions. Data that has not been logically ordered is difficult to understand and may lead to confusion and an inability to find the true facts of a case. When the information is organized and presented in a way that is easier to follow, solutions to the problems are more identifiable because all the relevant details can be processed in a logical progression. When a case is just beginning, information will come to the officer in a disorganized way; it will be up to the officer to find all the facts of the case and reorganize them so they can be better used and understood. It is also important to have this logical progression of facts in order for others who may not have collected the data to be able to read about and understand the case at any moment.

Common instances of scrambled facts come in the form of witness statements. Several factors, such as the high emotional states of the witnesses, their lack of factual details, or the sheer number of witnesses involved, contribute to the sometimes disorganized data an officer receives. When obtaining information from a witness, an officer needs to first identify the facts of the case. True facts can be validated from multiple sources; they also are spoken with more confidence and relate to specific, objective details over emotional experiences. Once the officer has identified all the facts in an incident, they can then begin to place the facts in logical order. It is helpful for the officer to progress in a linear way, starting with what happened first and providing a progression of events up until the time of reporting. Once the facts follow a forward trajectory, they can be better used to recreate the scene and progress the information into a conclusion.

Finding the Perpetrator from a Description of Suspects Given Information About an Arrested Person

When someone is arrested, information about their appearance and the crime or crimes they are being accused of is recorded. If the suspect in a case is still unknown, officers will most likely arrest multiple people. It is then the officer's job to determine which suspect is the culprit based on descriptions and information about those who have been arrested. Information provided to the officer may be in the form of a sketch or image, but often an officer will have to interpret written or spoken words used to describe the perpetrator. The officer will need to know how to best use this information to form an image of what the perpetrator may look like and to choose the corresponding person from a group of arrested suspects.

When processing information about an arrested person, the officer needs to first identify the key details that describe how the perpetrator may look. It is important to focus on descriptions that are unique and, if possible, character defining, that may help single the individual out from a group of similar-looking individuals. An officer should be careful of general descriptions, such as "tall" or "old," that are imprecise and can be relative to the individual who gave the information and focus on descriptions that can be easily visually recognizable. The officer should be able to form a detailed mental image of what they believe the culprit looks like based on the descriptions given. Then, when presented with those

arrested, the officer can use this mental image to match which person they believe to be the perpetrator. However, an officer should never guess; if no arrests match the descriptions or lack distinctive details given about the perpetrator, more information will need to be gathered before a final decision should be made.

Finding the Most Appropriate Response to Police Scenarios

A police scenario can be any number of instances that are related to a case. An officer needs to be ready to make the most appropriate responses based on a combination of their training and reasoning abilities. An officer's actions should not only help to solve cases but should be made to first and foremost ensure the safety of those involved. Each police scenario will be different, so it may be difficult sometimes to decide what the correct course of action might be. Decisions also need to be made quickly in the event a scenario necessitates an immediate response. An officer will also be required to analyze and interpret data involved from multiple sources to fully understand other situations to make informed conclusions.

The first step to finding appropriate responses for a police scenario requires the collection and analyzation of data so the officer can be properly informed on the situation. The most useful data will be the honest facts, and therefore details will need to be researched to confirm the veracity of the data. If a more immediate action is needed, the officer will have to pay close attention to all the surrounding details and take note of anyone who is in immediate danger. Actions must be backed up based on the facts of the case later. After examining the details, an officer should think of several different actions that could be taken. These options should be contrasted with each other to determine which action would best fit the situation. The final decision should be the one that most conforms to the law and is the safest course of action to prevent danger in the field.

Identifying the Most and Least Meaningful Details in a Police Scenario

A scenario can involve a web of different and often conflicting sets of details. It is important for an officer to be able to identify the most and least meaningful details of a police scenario in order to focus on the information that will be the most helpful to solving a case. Although it is important to take note of as many details as possible when first encountering a case, in the long run, too many details for a given scenario will cause confusion if they are not vetted and organized. Focusing on finding the most and least meaningful details divides the information into what is the most relevant to the situation and what is superfluous to the case as a whole.

To discover which details are the most meaningful, it is important to first focus on the objective facts of the case. An officer should determine the beginning, middle, and end of the event; look for details that can be verified, such as time of day or objects involved; and value the information that is the most irrefutable, such as pictures or video of a scene. The credibility of each source should also be researched; the most credible information will be free from frequent changes of thought or details and will be the most understandable or logical in relation to the scenario. The most meaningful details will also be frequently repeated, appearing in more than one source. The officer should determine what the frame of mind may have been like for those involved and how that might affect the information they have given. The least meaningful details in a police scenario will be the lies. It is important for the officer to spot where the untruthful information is and identify why it does not correlate with other data examined. Details that have no relation to the people or objects involved in the case are not very meaningful and should be set aside when organizing data into a complete case, whereas the most important details should be made to stand out.

Filling in Police Forms

Police forms are used by officers to organize information in a set way that can be easily interpreted by anyone who comes into contact with the information. This is done to set a standard behind all information reported for consistency of documentation. Forms will contain details related to an incident and will be used as a way to relay information about a case internally between parties. A police officer needs to be familiar with what these forms look like and the protocol for filling in blank reports or answering questions from a filled-in form. This way, they are able to not only file their own forms but to read and interpret the forms filled out by another officer.

Most information regarding an incident that is not directly witnessed will come to an officer in the form of a written incident description. It will then be the officer's job to use this written description to fill out a blank police department form. The form will help lay the information out in a way that others in the police department have been trained to interpret. There will be separate sections pertaining to different details of an event or crime. An officer should look at the headings of the forms to determine what information to provide for each section, being as detailed as possible without providing too much unimportant information. The written description should not simply be copied over to the police form. The officer will need to interpret which data is the most important and how this data can be used to solve the case. Then, the officer will have to be able to read these forms to answer questions about an incident. Details should be able to be quickly spotted with the form because they will be laid out in a familiar way. Once the officer has familiarized themselves with the layout of the form, they can easily go to the specific section that contains the data needed to answer a question.

Applying Police Policies

It is important for an officer to completely understand the written details of any case they may be working on. Police policies have been put in place to create a method for examining and interpreting data presented to an officer. When an officer applies these police policies, they have a better chance of completely comprehending the case and can make better use of the data presented. Having the most important details is not enough if the officer cannot understand and use these details to make the most informed decisions. An officer should read all the details of an incident to have a clear understanding of each case that is presented to them. Although there may not be an objectively right way to interpret data, when it comes to the law, the most accurate interpretation will be the one that most coincides with the written law. Police policies are the tools an officer will use to interpret information by this standard of the law.

To start applying police policies to given situations, an officer needs to have a clear understanding of the policies of their local office. The officer should study the law definitions and be able to relate incidents to specific crimes as they are defined in text. Having a clear understanding of the laws in their area is the first step to applying these policies to specific cases. Once a thorough understanding of the law has been established, an officer should read and reread each report of an incident brought to them until they can form as clear a picture of the scene as possible. Then, the officer can start to draw comparisons to what they have read about the law, and specific police policies can be applied to the situation.

Frequency of Information Questions

Some of the most useful information involved in a case will come directly from witnesses. However, not all witnesses will give completely accurate information that can be used to solve the crime. It will be up

to the officer to determine what information is factual and which witnesses are giving the most accurate reports of the incident.

When determining which witness is giving the most factual details of a case, there are a few factors the officer can immediately determine, such as if the witness was actually there at the time of the crime or the amount of details a witness actually observed. If the witness was too far away to see anything important or if they were not directly involved in the case, their information will most likely not be worth much attention. An officer should also take into consideration how much time has passed between the crime and the questioning of the witness; if more time has elapsed, the information may not be remembered as clearly. After the witness's relation to the scene of the crime is determined, the officer can then interpret the confidence and completeness of their responses to determine which is the most truthful. True statements will be made confidently and stated in a way that can be clearly understood. True information will also appear frequently in more than one witness's testimony. If details about a case are repeated in the same way by multiple witnesses, the officer knows the information is most likely true. The witness who is telling the truth will be the one who can be backed up by other sources of evidence as well. The officer should ask about key details they already know to be true to see how the witness responds. The witness who is the most truthful will be the one who can back up their story with factual data.

Practice Questions

1. WITNESS STATEMENT: It was late at night, and a man was running very fast up the street near where I live. I also saw him a little earlier at the store and then at my neighbor's house. He went inside, but I assumed he was invited. After that is when I heard the loud sound.

Which of the following details in the witness's statement happened first?
    a. A man was seen running quickly up a street.
    b. A man is seen entering a house next to the witness.
    c. The witness sees the man at a store.
    d. A loud sound is heard by the witness.

2. A witness hears gunshots outside of their apartment, followed by screeching tires. Cries and moans of pain are heard nearby. What is the logical outcome of this scenario?
    a. There was a car crash.
    b. Something was stolen.
    c. There was a parade.
    d. Someone was shot, and the culprit's car sped away.

3. A man is reported to have been assaulted during a large bar fight. Which of the following information would MOST help identify the culprit?
    a. How tall he is
    b. Whether he has any visual bruises or scars
    c. His age
    d. What he was wearing

4. A man in proximity to a patrolling officer is reported to have robbed a local liquor store. There have been reports of gunshots. What would be the MOST appropriate response to this scenario?
    a. Approach the suspect.
    b. Call for backup.
    c. Ask the store clerk for more details.
    d. Ignore the report and continue patrolling.

5. An officer is called to the scene of a car accident. Upon arrival, the two drivers are seen arguing loudly, disputing the cause. What would be the MOST appropriate response to this scenario?
    a. Arrest both parties.
    b. Call for backup.
    c. Ask to hear and record both stories.
    d. Subdue whoever appears to be physically stronger.

Answer Explanations

1. C: By paying close attention to the witness's details, the events described can be reorganized in a logical order as the following: A man is seen at a store; he is then seen entering a house next to the witness; he runs out of the house up the street; and finally, a load noise is heard.

2. D: The logical outcome is that someone was shot and the culprit sped away. There were no indications of stolen items as reported by the witness (Choice *A*), no car crash–specific sounds were heard (Choice *B*), and a parade (Choice *C*) would be highly unlikely to sound the way the witness describes.

3. B: The most helpful detail would be visual bruises or scars because the culprit would most likely still have evidence of being in the large fight related to the case. Choices *A* and *C*, people of similar heights and ages, may be arrested as suspects, making it hard to visually determine the culprit using only this information. Choice *D,* what he was wearing, can be changed too easily to be useful in a lot of situations as well.

4. B: Any time the officer feels there may be danger involved, they should always call for backup. In this scenario, the gunshots indicate that the suspect may be armed, so approaching him alone (Choice *A*) may be unsafe. However, waiting to ask the store clerk for details (Choice *B*) or ignoring the crime (Choice *D*) may allow the suspect to escape.

5. C: The most appropriate response for the officer would be to record both parties' accounts of the incident. Although the drivers are described as being loud, the situation has not escalated to a dangerous level, and therefore arrest (Choice *A*), backup (Choice *B*), and force (Choice *D*) are not warranted.

Practice Test

Spelling

Directions: In the following sentences, choose the correct spelling of the missing word.

1. A non-violent breach of a law to bring about social change is called civil _____.
   a. disobidiance.
   b. disobedense.
   c. disobedience.
   d. disobediance.

2. After graduating from the Police Academy, you will be assigned to a _____.
   a. pricinct.
   b. precint.
   c. precinct.
   d. presinct.

3. Becoming a police officer is a great _____ to serve your community.
   a. oppurtinity
   b. opportunity
   c. opportinity
   d. oppurtunity

4. I _____ spilled coffee on my desk.
   a. acidentally
   b. assidentilly
   c. accidentilly
   d. accidentally

5. Your excellent work shows how _____ you are to the job.
   a. comited
   b. comitted
   c. commited
   d. committed

6. My flushed cheeks gave away my _____.
   a. embarassmint.
   b. embarrasment.
   c. embarrissment.
   d. embarrassment.

7. We have the lowest price, _____.
   a. guarenteed.
   b. guaranted.
   c. guarinteed.
   d. guaranteed.

8. Though baseball is my favorite sport, I _____ play golf.
    a. occasionaly
    b. occasionally
    c. ocassionally
    d. occassionaly

9. The *New York Journal* has _____ endorsed Andrew Walter for Congress.
    a. explicitally
    b. explicitly
    c. explicitely
    d. explicately

10. A _____ approach to cooking will ensure that your meals are healthy and delicious.
    a. conscientios
    b. concientious
    c. conscientious
    d. consciencious

11. I'm _____ looking forward to my vacation this year.
    a. definitly
    b. definitely
    c. defenitely
    d. definately

12. I hope that scientists are able to prove the _____ of aliens.
    a. existanse
    b. esixtinse
    c. existense
    d. existence

13. _____ speaking, our operating system is one of the best on the market.
    a. Technicaly
    b. Technicilly
    c. Technically
    d. Technikcally

14. When in need of advice on a case, I consult with my _____.
    a. sergeant.
    b. sergant.
    c. saergant.
    d. seargeant.

15. The car was _____ new when she purchased it.
    a. practicilly
    b. practicaly
    c. practikally
    d. practically

Enforcement Vocabulary

Directions: Read each sentence carefully and select the answer that is closest in meaning to the <u>underlined</u> word. Use prefix/suffix definitions and context clues to help eliminate incorrect answers.

1. Only one of the thieves who robbed the jewelry store was caught since his <u>accomplice</u> got away.
   a. Roommate
   b. Brother
   c. Partner
   d. Manager

2. The congressman denied the <u>allegation</u> that he'd voted in favor of the bill in exchange for a campaign donation.
   a. Claim
   b. Reptile
   c. Highway
   d. Interrogation

3. During the <u>arraignment</u> in front of the judge, Tommy pleaded not guilty to driving under the influence of alcohol.
   a. Wedding
   b. Proceeding
   c. Bouquet
   d. Conclusion

4. The violent offender was convicted of <u>battery</u> for using a baseball bat to strike his victim.
   a. Voltage
   b. Assault
   c. Flattery
   d. Arson

5. The gang members in Shelly's neighborhood tried to <u>coerce</u> her into selling drugs, but she refused to be bullied.
   a. Pay
   b. Discourage
   c. Gender
   d. Pressure

6. The company treasurer was found guilty of <u>embezzling</u> $50,000 from the company's bank account to pay for the remodeling of his home.
   a. Bedazzling
   b. Stealing
   c. Decorating
   d. Borrowing

7. The judge <u>exonerated</u> Susan of all charges, so she left the courtroom a free woman.
   a. Cleared
   b. Executed
   c. Tried
   d. Convicted

8. When officers arrived on the scene of the deadly crash, they learned there had been one <u>fatality</u>.
   a. Birth
   b. Attraction
   c. Death
   d. Celebration

9. The unsuspecting art collector didn't realize the painting was a <u>forgery</u> until after it was appraised, so she became the 13th victim of the con artist.
   a. Antique
   b. Operation
   c. Sculpture
   d. Fake

10. The criminals wore gloves so they wouldn't leave behind any <u>latent</u> fingerprints.
    a. Hidden
    b. Painted
    c. Vinyl
    d. Visible

11. The state declared a <u>moratorium</u> on executions after new evidence cleared one death row inmate of his crime.
    a. Funeral
    b. Postponement
    c. Speech
    d. Hospitalization

12. The witness said the <u>perpetrator</u> wore a black ski mask and a blonde wig during the home invasion.
    a. Model
    b. Student
    c. Criminal
    d. Dancer

13. Though Miss Johnson swore to tell the truth under oath, she actually tried to <u>prevaricate</u> and claimed she didn't remember any details.
    a. Steal
    b. Impregnate
    c. Lie
    d. Confess

14. The city's first responders must follow <u>protocol</u> when handling calls for cases of domestic violence.
    a. Guidelines
    b. Internist
    c. Requests
    d. Evidence

15. After the riot broke out, officers had to use strong measures to <u>quell</u> the angry crowd.
    a. Wave
    b. Count
    c. Incite
    d. Calm

Reading Comprehension

Directions for questions 1–9: Read the statement or passage and then choose the best answer to the question. Answer the question based on what is stated or implied in the statement or passage.

1. There are two major kinds of cameras on the market right now for amateur photographers. Camera enthusiasts can either purchase a digital single-lens reflex camera (DSLR) camera or a compact system camera (CSC). The main difference between a DSLR and a CSC is that the DSLR has a full-sized sensor, which means it fits in a much larger body. The CSC uses a mirrorless system, which makes for a lighter, smaller camera. While both take quality pictures, the DSLR generally has better picture quality due to the larger sensor. CSCs still take very good quality pictures and are more convenient to carry than a DSLR. This makes the CSC an ideal choice for the amateur photographer looking to step up from a point-and-shoot camera.

What is the main difference between the DSLR and CSC?
    a. The picture quality is better in the DSLR.
    b. The CSC is less expensive than the DSLR.
    c. The DSLR is a better choice for amateur photographers.
    d. The DSLR's larger sensor makes it a bigger camera than the CSC.

2. When selecting a career path, it's important to explore the various options available. Many students entering college may shy away from a major because they don't know much about it. For example, many students won't opt for a career as an actuary, because they aren't exactly sure what it entails. They would be missing out on a career that is very lucrative and in high demand. Actuaries work in the insurance field and assess risks and premiums. The average salary of an actuary is $100,000 per year. Another career option students may avoid, due to lack of knowledge of the field, is a hospitalist. This is a physician that specializes in the care of patients in a hospital, as opposed to those seen in private practices. The average salary of a hospitalist is upwards of $200,000. It pays to do some digging and find out more about these lesser-known career fields.

What is an actuary?
    a. A doctor who works in a hospital.
    b. The same as a hospitalist.
    c. An insurance agent who works in a hospital.
    d. A person who assesses insurance risks and premiums.

3. Hard water occurs when rainwater mixes with minerals from rock and soil. Hard water has a high mineral count, including calcium and magnesium. The mineral deposits from hard water can stain hard surfaces in bathrooms and kitchens as well as clog pipes. Hard water can stain dishes, ruin clothes, and reduce the life of any appliances it touches, such as hot water heaters, washing machines, and humidifiers.

One solution is to install a water softener to reduce the mineral content of water, but this can be costly. Running vinegar through pipes and appliances and using vinegar to clean hard surfaces can also help with mineral deposits.

From this passage, what can be concluded?
    a. Hard water can cause a lot of problems for homeowners.
    b. Calcium is good for pipes and hard surfaces.
    c. Water softeners are easy to install.
    d. Vinegar is the only solution to hard water problems.

4. Coaches of kids' sports teams are increasingly concerned about the behavior of parents at games. Parents are screaming and cursing at coaches, officials, players, and other parents. Physical fights have even broken out at games. Parents need to be reminded that coaches are volunteers, giving up their time and energy to help kids develop in their chosen sport. The goal of kids' sports teams is to learn and develop skills, but it's also to have fun. When parents are out of control at games and practices, it takes the fun out of the sport.

From this passage, what can be concluded?
    a. Coaches are modeling good behavior for kids.
    b. Organized sports are not good for kids.
    c. Parents' behavior at their kids' games needs to change.
    d. Parents and coaches need to work together.

5. While scientists aren't entirely certain why tornadoes form, they have some clues into the process. Tornadoes are dangerous funnel clouds that occur during a large thunderstorm. When warm, humid air near the ground meets cold, dry air from above, a column of the warm air can be drawn up into the clouds. Winds at different altitudes blowing at different speeds make the column of air rotate. As the spinning column of air picks up speed, a funnel cloud is formed. This funnel cloud moves rapidly and haphazardly. Rain and hail inside the cloud cause it to touch down, creating a tornado. Tornadoes move in a rapid and unpredictable pattern, making them extremely destructive and dangerous. Scientists continue to study tornadoes to improve radar detection and warning times.

The main purpose of this passage is to do which of the following?
    a. Show why tornadoes are dangerous.
    b. Explain how a tornado forms.
    c. Compare thunderstorms to tornadoes.
    d. Explain what to do in the event of a tornado.

6. Many people are unsure of exactly how the digestive system works. Digestion begins in the mouth where teeth grind up food and saliva break it down, making it easier for the body to absorb. Next, the food moves to the esophagus, and it is pushed into the stomach. The stomach is where food is stored and broken down further by acids and digestive enzymes, preparing it for passage into the intestines. The small intestine is where the nutrients are taken from food and passed into the blood stream. Other essential organs like the liver, gall bladder, and pancreas aid the stomach in breaking down food and absorbing nutrients. Finally, food waste is passed into the large intestine where it is eliminated by the body.

The purpose of this passage is to do which of the following?
a. Explain how the liver works.
b. Show why it is important to eat healthy foods.
c. Explain how the digestive system works.
d. Show how nutrients are absorbed by the small intestine.

7. Osteoporosis is a medical condition that occurs when the body loses bone or makes too little bone. This can lead to brittle, fragile bones that easily break. Bones are already porous, and when osteoporosis sets in, the spaces in bones become much larger, causing them to weaken. Both men and women can contract osteoporosis, though it is most common in women over age 50. Loss of bone can be silent and progressive, so it is important to be proactive in prevention of the disease.

The main purpose of this passage is to do which of the following?
a. Discuss some of the ways people contract osteoporosis.
b. Describe different treatment options for those with osteoporosis.
c. Explain how to prevent osteoporosis.
d. Define osteoporosis.

8. Vacationers looking for a perfect experience should opt out of Disney parks and try a trip on Disney Cruise Lines. While a park offers rides, characters, and show experiences, it also includes long lines, often very hot weather, and enormous crowds. A Disney Cruise, on the other hand, is a relaxing, luxurious vacation that includes many of the same experiences as the parks, minus the crowds and lines. The cruise has top-notch food, maid service, water slides, multiple pools, Broadway-quality shows, and daily character experiences for kids. There are also many activities, such as bingo, trivia contests, and dance parties that can entertain guests of all ages. The cruise even stops at Disney's private island for a beach barbecue with characters, waterslides, and water sports. Those looking for the Disney experience without the hassle should book a Disney cruise.

The main purpose of this passage is to do which of the following?
a. Explain how to book a Disney cruise.
b. Show what Disney parks have to offer.
c. Show why Disney parks are expensive.
d. Compare Disney parks to the Disney cruise.

9. As summer approaches, drowning incidents will increase. Drowning happens very quickly and silently. Most people assume that drowning is easy to spot, but a person who is drowning doesn't make noise or wave their arms. Instead, they will have their head back and their mouth open, with just the face out of the water. A person who is truly in danger of drowning is not able to wave their arms in the air or move much at all. Recognizing these signs of drowning can prevent tragedy.

The main purpose of this passage is to do which of the following?
a. Explain the dangers of swimming.
b. Show how to identify the signs of drowning.
c. Explain how to be a lifeguard.
d. Compare the signs of drowning.

The next three questions are based on the following passage.

Christopher Columbus is often credited for discovering America. This is incorrect. First, it is impossible to "discover" something where people already live; however, Christopher Columbus did explore places in the New World that were previously untouched by Europe, so the term "explorer" would be more accurate. Another correction must be made, as well: Christopher Columbus was not the first European explorer to reach the present day Americas! Rather, it was Leif Erikson who first came to the New World and contacted the natives, nearly five hundred years before Christopher Columbus.

Leif Erikson, the son of Erik the Red (a famous Viking outlaw and explorer in his own right), was born in either 970 or 980, depending on which historian you seek. His own family, though, did not raise Leif, which was a Viking tradition. Instead, one of Erik's prisoners taught Leif reading and writing, languages, sailing, and weaponry. At age 12, Leif was considered a man and returned to his family. He killed a man during a dispute shortly after his return, and the council banished the Erikson clan to Greenland.

In 999, Leif left Greenland and traveled to Norway where he would serve as a guard to King Olaf Tryggvason. It was there that he became a convert to Christianity. Leif later tried to return home with the intention of taking supplies and spreading Christianity to Greenland, however his ship was blown off course and he arrived in a strange new land: present day Newfoundland, Canada.

When he finally returned to his adopted homeland Greenland, Leif consulted with a merchant who had also seen the shores of this previously unknown land we now know as Canada. The son of the legendary Viking explorer then gathered a crew of 35 men and set sail. Leif became the first European to touch foot in the New World as he explored present-day Baffin Island and Labrador, Canada. His crew called the land Vinland since it was plentiful with grapes.

During their time in present-day Newfoundland, Leif's expedition made contact with the natives whom they referred to as Skraelings (which translates to "wretched ones" in Norse). There are several secondhand accounts of their meetings. Some contemporaries described trade between the peoples. Other accounts describe clashes where the Skraelings defeated the Viking explorers with long spears, while still others claim the Vikings dominated the natives. Regardless of the circumstances, it seems that the Vikings made contact of some kind. This happened around 1000, nearly five hundred years before Columbus famously sailed the ocean blue.

Eventually, in 1003, Leif set sail for home and arrived at Greenland with a ship full of timber. In 1020, seventeen years later, the legendary Viking died. Many believe that Leif Erikson should receive more credit for his contributions in exploring the New World.

10. Which of the following is an opinion, rather than historical fact, expressed by the author?
    a. Leif Erikson was definitely the son of Erik the Red; however, historians debate the year of his birth.
    b. Leif Erikson's crew called the land Vinland since it was plentiful with grapes.
    c. Leif Erikson deserves more credit for his contributions in exploring the New World.
    d. Leif Erikson explored the Americas nearly five hundred years before Christopher Columbus.

11. Which of the following most accurately describes the author's main conclusion?
    a. Leif Erikson is a legendary Viking explorer.
    b. Leif Erikson deserves more credit for exploring America hundreds of years before Columbus.
    c. Spreading Christianity motivated Leif Erikson's expeditions more than any other factor.
    d. Leif Erikson contacted the natives nearly five hundred years before Columbus.

12. Which of the following can be logically inferred from the passage?
    a. The Vikings disliked exploring the New World.
    b. Leif Erikson's banishment from Iceland led to his exploration of present-day Canada.
    c. Leif Erikson never shared his stories of exploration with the King of Norway.
    d. Historians have difficulty definitively pinpointing events in the Vikings' history.

This article discusses the famous poet and playwright William Shakespeare. Read it and answer questions 13–16.

People who argue that William Shakespeare is not responsible for the plays attributed to his name are known as anti-Stratfordians (from the name of Shakespeare's birthplace, Stratford-upon-Avon). The most common anti-Stratfordian claim is that William Shakespeare simply was not educated enough or from a high enough social class to have written plays overflowing with references to such a wide range of subjects like history, the classics, religion, and international culture. William Shakespeare was the son of a glove-maker, he only had a basic grade school education, and he never set foot outside of England—so how could he have produced plays of such sophistication and imagination? How could he have written in such detail about historical figures and events, or about different cultures and locations around Europe? According to anti-Stratfordians, the depth of knowledge contained in Shakespeare's plays suggests a well-traveled writer from a wealthy background with a university education, not a countryside writer like Shakespeare. But in fact, there is not much substance to such speculation, and most anti-Stratfordian arguments can be refuted with a little background about Shakespeare's time and upbringing.

First of all, those who doubt Shakespeare's authorship often point to his common birth and brief education as stumbling blocks to his writerly genius. Although it is true that Shakespeare did not come from a noble class, his father was a very *successful* glove-maker and his mother was from a very wealthy land-owning family—so while Shakespeare may have had a country upbringing, he was certainly from a well-off family and would have been educated accordingly. Also, even though he did not attend university, grade school education in Shakespeare's time was actually quite rigorous and exposed students to classic drama through writers like Seneca and Ovid. It is

not unreasonable to believe that Shakespeare received a very solid foundation in poetry and literature from his early schooling.

Next, anti-Stratfordians tend to question how Shakespeare could write so extensively about countries and cultures he had never visited before (for instance, several of his most famous works like *Romeo and Juliet* and *The Merchant of Venice* were set in Italy, on the opposite side of Europe!). But again, this criticism does not hold up under scrutiny. For one thing, Shakespeare was living in London, a bustling metropolis of international trade, the most populous city in England, and a political and cultural hub of Europe. In the daily crowds of people, Shakespeare would certainly have been able to meet travelers from other countries and hear firsthand accounts of life in their home country. And, in addition to the influx of information from world travelers, this was also the age of the printing press, a jump in technology that made it possible to print and circulate books much more easily than in the past. This also allowed for a freer flow of information across different countries, allowing people to read about life and ideas from throughout Europe. One needn't travel the continent in order to learn and write about its culture.

13. Which sentence contains the author's thesis?
    a. People who argue that William Shakespeare is not responsible for the plays attributed to his name are known as anti-Stratfordians.
    b. But in fact, there is not much substance to such speculation, and most anti-Stratfordian arguments can be refuted with a little background about Shakespeare's time and upbringing.
    c. It is not unreasonable to believe that Shakespeare received a very solid foundation in poetry and literature from his early schooling.
    d. Next, anti-Stratfordians tend to question how Shakespeare could write so extensively about countries and cultures he had never visited before.

14. In the first paragraph, "How could he have written in such detail about historical figures and events, or about different cultures and locations around Europe?" is an example of which of the following?
    a. Hyperbole
    b. Onomatopoeia
    c. Rhetorical question
    d. Appeal to authority

15. How does the author respond to the claim that Shakespeare was not well-educated because he did not attend university?
    a. By insisting upon Shakespeare's natural genius.
    b. By explaining grade school curriculum in Shakespeare's time.
    c. By comparing Shakespeare with other uneducated writers of his time.
    d. By pointing out that Shakespeare's wealthy parents probably paid for private tutors.

16. The word "bustling" in the third paragraph most nearly means which of the following?
    a. Busy
    b. Foreign
    c. Expensive
    d. Undeveloped

The next article is for questions 17–19.

It has recently been brought to my attention that most people believe that 75% of your body heat is lost through your head. I had certainly heard this before, and am not going to attempt to say I didn't believe it when I first heard it. It is natural to be gullible to anything said with enough authority. But the "fact" that the majority of your body heat is lost through your head is a lie.

Let me explain. Heat loss is proportional to surface area exposed. An elephant loses a great deal more heat than an anteater because it has a much greater surface area than an anteater. Each cell has mitochondria that produce energy in the form of heat, and it takes a lot more energy to run an elephant than an anteater.

So, each part of your body loses its proportional amount of heat in accordance with its surface area. The human torso probably loses the most heat, though the legs lose a significant amount as well. Some people have asked, "Why does it feel so much warmer when you cover your head than when you don't?" Well, that's because your head, because it is not clothed, is losing a lot of heat while the clothing on the rest of your body provides insulation. If you went outside with a hat and pants but no shirt, not only would you look silly, but your heat loss would be significantly greater because so much more of you would be exposed. So, if given the choice to cover your chest or your head in the cold, choose the chest. It could save your life.

17. Why does the author compare elephants and anteaters?
    a. To express an opinion.
    b. To give an example that helps clarify the main point.
    c. To show the differences between them.
    d. To persuade why one is better than the other.

18. Which of the following best describes the tone of the passage?
    a. Harsh
    b. Angry
    c. Casual
    d. Indifferent

19. The author appeals to which branch of rhetoric to prove their case?
    a. Factual evidence
    b. Emotion
    c. Ethics and morals
    d. Author qualification

Questions 20–22 are based on the following passage:

The town of Alexandria, Virginia was founded in 1749. Between the years 1810 and 1861, this thriving seaport was the ideal location for slave owners such as Joseph Bruin, Henry Hill, Isaac Franklin, and John Armfield to build several slave trade office structures, including slave holding areas. After 1830, when the manufacturing-based economy slowed down in Virginia, slaves were traded to plantations in the Deep South, in Alabama, Mississippi, and Louisiana. Joseph Bruin, one of the most notorious of the slave traders operating in Alexandria, alone purchased hundreds of slaves from 1844 to 1861. Harriet Beecher Stowe claimed that the horrible slave traders mentioned in her novel, *Uncle Tom's Cabin*, are reminiscent of the coldhearted Joseph Bruin. The Franklin and Armfield Office was known as one of the largest slave trading companies

in the country up to the end of the Civil War period. Slaves, waiting to be traded, were held in a two-story slave pen built behind the Franklin and Armfield Office structure on Duke Street in Alexandria. Yet, many people fought to thwart these traders and did everything they could to rescue and free slaves. Two Christian African American slave sisters, with the help of northern abolitionists who bought their freedom, escaped Bruin's plan to sell them into southern prostitution. In 1861, Joseph Bruin was captured and imprisoned and his property confiscated. The Bruin Slave Jail became the Fairfax County courthouse until 1865. The original Franklin and Armfield Office building still stands in Virginia and is registered in the National Register of Historic Places. The Bruin Slave Jail is still standing on Duke Street in Alexandria, but is not open to the public. The history of the slave trading enterprise is preserved and presented to the public by the Northern Virginia Urban League.

20. Based on the above passage, which of the following statements about the town of Alexandria are true?

a. Alexandria was a seaport town, which could not prosper, even with the advent of a slave trade business, because the manufacturing industry was not enough to stabilize the economy.

b. Slave traders such as Joseph Bruin, Henry Hill, Isaac Franklin, and John Armfield rented both slave trade office buildings and slave holding buildings from landlords of Old Town, Alexandria.

c. For over fifteen years, Joseph Bruin, a notorious slave trader, probably the one characterized in *Uncle Tom's Cabin*, bought hundreds of slaves with the intention of sending the purchased slaves to southern states such as Alabama, Mississippi, and Louisiana.

d. The Bruin Slave Jail is open to the public; the building is located in downtown Alexandria, and still stands in Virginia. The jail is registered in the National Register of Historic Places. The history of the slave trading enterprise is preserved and presented to the public by the Northern Virginia Urban League.

21. The passage about the Alexandria slave trade business suggests that which of the following statements can be regarded as true?

a. The lucrative seaport town of Alexandria was supported by successful slave trade businesses of men like Joseph Bruin, Henry Hill, Isaac Franklin, and John Armfield, who bought slaves and sold them to the plantations in the Deep South.

b. Joseph Bruin, a highly respected Alexandrian businessman, ran a slave trade business in downtown Alexandria, until the business closed its doors at the end of the Civil War.

c. The Franklin and Armfield Office was built by Isaac Franklin and John Armfield. Slaves, waiting to be traded, were held in a four-story slave pen built behind the Franklin and Armfield Office structure on Duke Street in Alexandria.

d. When the Confederate Army positioned its command in Alexandria, and closed slave traders' businesses, the Franklin and Armfield slave pen became the Fairfax County courthouse and was used to hold Union soldiers.

22. Which of the following statements best illustrates the author's intended main point or thesis?

a. Two Christian African American slave sisters, with the help of northern abolitionists who bought their freedom, escaped Bruin's plan to sell them into southern prostitution.

b. The town of Alexandria, a thriving seaport founded in 1749, was the location for several lucrative slave trading companies from 1810 to 1861.

c. After the start of the Civil War, Joseph Bruin was captured and his jail was no longer used for his slave trade business.

d. The Bruin Slave Jail is still standing on Duke Street in Alexandria, but is not open to the public.

Questions 23–25 are based on the following passage:

Becoming a successful leader in today's industry, government, and nonprofit sectors requires more than a high intelligence quotient (IQ). Emotional Intelligence (EI) includes developing the ability to know one's own emotions, to regulate impulses and emotions, and to use interpersonal communication skills with ease while dealing with other people. A combination of knowledge, skills, abilities, and mature emotional intelligence (EI) reflects the most effective leadership recipe. Successful leaders sharpen more than their talents and IQ levels; they practice the basic features of emotional intelligence. Some of the hallmark traits of a competent, emotionally intelligent leader include self-efficacy, drive, determination, collaboration, vision, humility, and openness to change. An unsuccessful leader exhibits opposite leadership traits: unclear directives, inconsistent vision and planning strategies, disrespect for followers, incompetence, and an uncompromising transactional leadership style. There are ways to develop emotional intelligence for the person who wants to improve his or her leadership style. For example, an emotionally intelligent leader creates an affirmative environment by incorporating collaborative activities, using professional development training for employee self-awareness, communicating clearly about the organization's vision, and developing a variety of resources for working with emotions. Building relationships outside the institution with leadership coaches and with professional development trainers can also help leaders who want to grow their leadership success. Leaders in today's work environment need to strive for a combination of skill, knowledge, and mature emotional intelligence to lead followers to success and to promote the vision and mission of their respective institutions.

23. The passage suggests that the term *emotional intelligence (EI)* can be defined as which of the following?

a. A combination of knowledge, skills, abilities, and mature emotional intelligence reflects the most effective EI leadership recipe.

b. An emotionally intelligent leader creates an affirmative environment by incorporating collaborative activities, using professional development training for employee self-awareness, communicating clearly about the organization's vision, and developing a variety of resources for working with emotions.

c. EI includes developing the ability to know one's own emotions, to regulate impulses and emotions, and to use interpersonal communication skills with ease while dealing with other people.

d. Becoming a successful leader in today's industry, government, and nonprofit sectors requires more than a high IQ.

24. According to the passage above, some of the characteristics of an unsuccessful leader include which of the following?

a. Talent, IQ level, and abilities

b. Humility, knowledge, and skills

c. Loud, demeaning actions toward female employees

d. Transactional leadership style

25. According to the passage above, which of the following must be true?

a. The leader exhibits a healthy work/life balance lifestyle.

b. The leader is uncompromising in transactional directives for all employees, regardless of status.

c. The leader learns to strategize using future trends analysis to create a five-year plan.

d. The leader uses a combination of skill, knowledge, and mature reasoning to make decisions.

Questions 26–28 are based on the following passage.

Learning how to write a ten-minute play may seem like a monumental task at first; but, if you follow a simple creative writing strategy, similar to writing a narrative story, you will be able to write a successful drama. The first step is to open your story as if it is a puzzle to be solved. This will allow the reader a moment to engage with the story and to mentally solve the story with you, the author. Immediately provide descriptive details that steer the main idea, the tone, and the mood according to the overarching theme you have in mind. For example, if the play is about something ominous, you may open Scene One with a thunderclap. Next, use dialogue to reveal the attitudes and personalities of each of the characters who have a key part in the unfolding story. Keep the characters off balance in some way to create interest and dramatic effect. Maybe what the characters say does not match what they do. Show images on stage to speed up the narrative; remember, one picture speaks a thousand words. As the play progresses, the protagonist must cross the point of no return in some way; this is the climax of the story. Then, as in a written story, you create a resolution to the life-changing event of the protagonist. Let the characters experience some kind of self-discovery that can be understood and appreciated by the patient audience. Finally, make sure all things come together in the end so that every detail in the play makes sense right before the curtain falls.

26. Based on the passage above, which of the following statements is FALSE?
    a. Writing a ten-minute play may seem like an insurmountable task.
    b. Providing descriptive details is not necessary until after the climax of the story line.
    c. Engaging the audience by jumping into the story line immediately helps the audience solve the story's developing ideas with you, the writer.
    d. Descriptive details give clues to the play's intended mood and tone.

27. In the passage above, the writer suggests that writing a ten-minute play is accessible for a novice playwright because of which of the following reasons?
    a. It took the author of the passage only one week to write their first play.
    b. The format follows similar strategies of writing a narrative story.
    c. There are no particular themes or points to unravel; a playwright can use a stream of consciousness style to write a play.
    d. Dialogue that reveals the characters' particularities is uncommonly simple to write.

28. Based on the passage above, which of the following is true?
    a. The class of eighth graders quickly learned that it is not that difficult to write a ten-minute play.
    b. The playwrights of the twenty-first century all use the narrative writing basic feature guide to outline their initial scripts.
    c. In order to follow a simple structure, a person can write a ten-minute play based on some narrative writing features.
    d. The most important part of writing a play is the time given to developing the characters and their personalities.

29. Technology has been invading cars for the last several years, but there are some new high tech trends that are pretty amazing. It is now standard in many car models to have a rear-view camera, hands-free phone and text, and a touch screen digital display. Music can be streamed from a paired cell phone, and some displays can even be programmed with a personal photo. Sensors beep to indicate there is something in the driver's path when reversing and changing lanes. Rain-sensing windshield wipers and lights are automatic, leaving the driver with little to do but watch the road and enjoy the ride. The next wave of technology will include cars that automatically parallel park, and a self-driving car is on the horizon. These technological advances make it a good time to be a driver.

It can be concluded from this paragraph that:
    a. Technology will continue to influence how cars are made.
    b. Windshield wipers and lights are always automatic.
    c. It is standard to have a rear-view camera in all cars.
    d. Technology has reached its peak in cars.

Directions for questions 30–39: For the questions that follow, two underlined sentences are followed by a question or statement. Read the sentences, then choose the best answer to the question or the best completion of the statement.

30. The NBA draft process is based on a lottery system among the teams who did not make the playoffs in the previous season to determine draft order. Only the top three draft picks are determined by the lottery.

What does the *second sentence* do?
    a. It contradicts the first.
    b. It supports the first.
    c. It restates information from the first.
    d. It offers a solution.

31. While many people use multiple social media sites, Facebook remains the most popular with more than one billion users. Instagram is rising in popularity and, with 100 million users, is now the most-used social media site.

What does the *second sentence* do?
    a. It expands on the first.
    b. It contradicts the first.
    c. It supports the first.
    d. It proposes a solution.

32. There are eight different phases of the moon, from full moon to new moon. One of the eight different moon phases is first quarter, commonly called a half moon.

What does the *second sentence* do?
    a. It provides an example.
    b. It contradicts the first.
    c. It states an effect.
    d. It offers a solution.

33. The terror attacks of September 11, 2001 have had many lasting effects on the United States. The Department of Homeland Security was created in late September 2001 in response to the terror attacks and became an official cabinet-level department in November of 2002.

What does the *second sentence* do?
    a. It contradicts the first.
    b. It restates the information from the first.
    c. It states an effect.
    d. It makes a contrast.

34. Annuals are plants that complete the life cycle in a single growing season. Perennials are plants that complete the life cycle in many growing seasons, dying in the winter and coming back each spring.

What does the *second sentence* do?
    a. It makes a contrast.
    b. It disputes the first sentence.
    c. It provides an example.
    d. It states an effect.

35. Personal computers can be subject to viruses and malware, which can lead to slow performance, loss of files, and overheating. Antivirus software is often sold along with a new PC to protect against viruses and malware.

What does the *second sentence* do?
    a. It makes a contrast.
    b. It provides an example.
    c. It restates the information from the first.
    d. It offers a solution.

36. Many companies tout their chicken as cage-free because the chickens are not confined to small wire cages. However, cage-free chickens are often crammed into buildings with thousands of other birds and never go outside in their short lifetime.

What does the *second sentence* do?
    a. It offers a solution.
    b. It provides an example.
    c. It disputes the first sentence.
    d. It states an effect.

37. Common core standards do not include the instruction of cursive handwriting. The next generation of students will not be able to read or write cursive handwriting.

What does the *second sentence* do?
    a. It offers a solution.
    b. It states an effect.
    c. It contradicts the first sentence.
    d. It restates the first sentence.

38. Air travel has changed significantly in the last ten years. Airlines are now offering pay-as-you-go perks, including no baggage fees, seat selection, and food and drinks on the flight to keep costs low.

What does the *second sentence* do?
    a. It states effects.
    b. It provides examples.
    c. It disputes the first sentence.
    d. It offers solutions.

39. Many people are unaware that fragrances and other chemicals in their favorite products are causing skin reactions and allergies. Surprisingly, many popular products contain ingredients that can cause skin allergies.

What does the *second sentence* do?
    a. It restates the first sentence.
    b. It provides examples.
    c. It contradicts the first sentence.
    d. It provides solutions.

Mathematics

1. Which is closest to 17.8×9.9?
    a. 140
    b. 180
    c. 200
    d. 350

2. A student gets an 85% on a test with 20 questions. How many answers did the student solve correctly?
    a. 15
    b. 16
    c. 17
    d. 18

3. Four people split a bill. The first person pays for $\frac{1}{5}$, the second person pays for $\frac{1}{4}$, and the third person pays for $\frac{1}{3}$. What fraction of the bill does the fourth person pay?
    a. $\frac{13}{60}$
    b. $\frac{47}{60}$
    c. $\frac{1}{4}$
    d. $\frac{4}{15}$

4. 6 is 30% of what number?
    a. 18
    b. 20
    c. 24
    d. 26

5. $3\frac{2}{3} - 1\frac{4}{5} =$

    a. $1\frac{13}{15}$

    b. $\frac{14}{15}$

    c. $2\frac{2}{3}$

    d. $\frac{4}{5}$

6. What is $\frac{420}{98}$ rounded to the nearest integer?

    a. 4

    b. 3

    c. 5

    d. 6

7. $4\frac{1}{3} + 3\frac{3}{4} =$

    a. $6\frac{5}{12}$

    b. $8\frac{1}{12}$

    c. $8\frac{2}{3}$

    d. $7\frac{7}{12}$

8. Five of six numbers have a sum of 25. The average of all six numbers is 6. What is the sixth number?

    a. 8

    b. 10

    c. 11

    d. 12

9. $52.3 \times 10^{-3} =$

    a. 0.00523

    b. 0.0523

    c. 0.523

    d. 523

10. If $\frac{5}{2} \div \frac{1}{3} = n$, then n is between:

    a. 5 and 7

    b. 7 and 9

    c. 9 and 11

    d. 3 and 5

11. A closet is filled with red, blue, and green shirts. If $\frac{1}{3}$ of the shirts are green and $\frac{2}{5}$ are red, what fraction of the shirts are blue?

    a. $\frac{4}{15}$

    b. $\frac{1}{5}$

    c. $\frac{7}{15}$

    d. $\frac{1}{2}$

12. Shawna buys $2\frac{1}{2}$ gallons of paint. If she uses $\frac{1}{3}$ of it on the first day, how much does she have left?

   a. $1\frac{5}{6}$ gallons

   b. $1\frac{1}{2}$ gallons

   c. $1\frac{2}{3}$ gallons

   d. 2 gallons

13. A dress costs $15. What is the total if tax is 8%?
   a. $15.08
   b. $16.20
   c. $15.15
   d. $16.50

14. If $x = .5$, what is the solution to the following equation? $2x + \frac{10}{x}$
   a. 7
   b. 6
   c. 22
   d. 21

15. What is 23.156 rounded to the nearest hundredth?
   a. 23.2
   b. 23.16
   c. 23.15
   d. 23.17

Grammar

1. Which of the following is a clearer way to describe the following phrase?
   "employee-manager relations improvement guide"

   a. A guide to employing better managers
   b. A guide to improving relations between managers and employees
   c. A relationship between employees, managers, and improvement
   d. An improvement in employees' and managers' use of guides

Read the sentences, and then answer the following question.

2. Polls show that more and more people in the U.S. distrust the government and view it as dysfunctional and corrupt. Every election, the same people are voted back into office.

Which word or words would best link these sentences?
   a. Not surprisingly,
   b. Understandably,
   c. And yet,
   d. Therefore,

3. Which of the following statements would make the best conclusion to an essay about civil rights activist Rosa Parks?

    a. On December 1, 1955, Rosa Parks refused to give up her bus seat to a white passenger, setting in motion the Montgomery bus boycott.

    b. Rosa Parks was a hero to many and came to symbolize the way that ordinary people could bring about real change in the Civil Rights Movement.

    c. Rosa Parks died in 2005 in Detroit, having moved from Montgomery shortly after the bus boycott.

    d. Rosa Parks' arrest was an early part of the Civil Rights Movement and helped lead to the passage of the Civil Rights Act of 1964.

Select the best version of the underlined part of the sentence. If you think the original sentence is best, choose the first answer.

4. Since <u>none of the furniture were delivered</u> on time, we have to move in at a later date.

    a. none of the furniture were delivered

    b. none of the furniture was delivered

    c. all of the furniture were delivered

    d. all of the furniture was delivered

5. <u>An important issues stemming from this meeting</u> is that we won't have enough time to meet all of the objectives.

    a. An important issues stemming from this meeting

    b. Important issue stemming from this meeting

    c. An important issue stemming from this meeting

    d. Important issues stemming from this meeting

6. There were many questions <u>about what causes the case to have gone cold</u>, but the detective wasn't willing to discuss it with reporters.

    a. about what causes the case to have gone cold

    b. about why the case is cold

    c. about what causes the case to go cold

    d. about why the case went cold

Directions for questions 12–16: Select the best version of the underlined part of the sentence. The first choice is the same as the original sentence. If you think the original sentence is best, choose the first answer.

7. The fact <u>the train set only includes four cars and one small track was a big disappointment</u> to my son.

    a. the train set only includes four cars and one small track was a big disappointment

    b. that the trains set only include four cars and one small track was a big disappointment

    c. that the train set only includes four cars and one small track was a big disappointment

    d. that the train set only includes four cars and one small track were a big disappointment

8. The rising popularity of the clean eating movement can be attributed <u>to the fact that experts say added sugars and chemicals in our food are to blame for the obesity epidemic.</u>

    a. to the fact that experts say added sugars and chemicals in our food are to blame for the obesity epidemic.

    b. in the facts that experts say added sugars and chemicals in our food are to blame for the obesity epidemic.

    c. to the fact that experts saying added sugars and chemicals in our food are to blame for the obesity epidemic.

    d. with the facts that experts say added sugars and chemicals in our food are to blame for the obesity epidemic.

9. She's looking for a suitcase that can fit all of her <u>clothes, shoes, accessory, and makeup.</u>

    a. clothes, shoes, accessory, and makeup.

    b. clothes, shoes, accessories, and makeup.

    c. clothes, shoes, accessories, and makeups.

    d. clothes, shoe, accessory, and makeup.

10. Shawn started taking guitar lessons <u>while he wanted to become a better musician.</u>

    a. while he wanted to become a better musician.

    b. because he wants to become a better musician.

    c. even though he wanted to become a better musician.

    d. because he wanted to become a better musician.

11. <u>Considering the recent rains we have had, it's a wonder</u> the plants haven't drowned.

    a. Considering the recent rains we have had, it's a wonder

    b. Consider the recent rains we have had, it's a wonder

    c. Considering for how much recent rain we have had, it's a wonder

    d. Considering, the recent rains we have had, it's a wonder

Directions for questions 17–20: Rewrite the sentence in your head following the directions given below. Keep in mind that your new sentence should be well written and should have essentially the same meaning as the original sentence.

12. There are many risks in firefighting, including smoke inhalation, exposure to hazardous materials, and oxygen deprivation, so firefighters are outfitted with many items that could save their lives, including a self-contained breathing apparatus.

Rewrite, beginning with <u>so firefighters.</u>

The next words will be which of the following?

    a. are exposed to lots of dangerous situations.

    b. need to be very careful on the job.

    c. wear life-saving protective gear.

    d. have very risky jobs.

13. Though social media sites like Facebook, Instagram, and Snapchat have become increasingly popular, experts warn that teen users are exposing themselves to many dangers such as cyberbullying and predators.

Rewrite, beginning with <u>experts warn that.</u>

The next words will be which of the following?
    a. Facebook is dangerous.
    b. they are growing in popularity.
    c. teens are using them too much.
    d. they can be dangerous for teens.

14. Student loan debt is at an all-time high, which is why many politicians are using this issue to gain the attention and votes of students, or anyone with student loan debt.

Rewrite, beginning with <u>Student loan debt is at an all-time high.</u>

The next words will be which of the following?
    a. because politicians want students' votes.
    b. , so politicians are using the issue to gain votes.
    c. , so voters are choosing politicians who care about this issue.
    d. , and politicians want to do something about it.

15. Seasoned runners often advise new runners to get fitted for better quality running shoes because new runners often complain about minor injuries like sore knees or shin splints.

Rewrite, beginning with <u>Seasoned runners often advise new runners to get fitted for better quality running shoes.</u>

The next words will be which of the following?
    a. to help them avoid minor injuries.
    b. because they know better.
    c. , so they can run further.
    d. to complain about running injuries.

Verbal Expression

1. Theft can be defined as the act of taking something from another person without permission. Which of the following police situations would apply to this definition?
    a. A wife reports that her husband threw a plate and hit her.
    b. A dog is reported missing.
    c. A man reports that the window of his car was broken and his jacket is missing from the car.
    d. A cat is stuck in a tree.

2. A man exposes his body without any clothing in a public restaurant during peak business hours. Which of the following definitions applies to the incident?
    a. Public indecency
    b. Domestic abuse
    c. Theft
    d. Drug possession

3. Officer Skylor is reading reports about crimes that occur in his patrol area.

> All drug deals reported occur between 19th Avenue and 45th Avenue, all house break-ins occur in the neighborhoods between Roosevelt and Van Buren, and all vehicle break-ins occur by the strip mall along Indian School Road.

> Most drug deals happen on Fridays, most house break-ins occur on Mondays, and most vehicle break-ins occur on Wednesdays.

> Most drug deals happen between 8:00 p.m. and midnight, most house break-ins occur between 10:00 a.m. and 2:00 p.m., and most vehicle break-ins occur between 5:00 p.m. and 9:00 p.m.

Officer Skylor will have the best chance of decreasing vehicle break-ins if he patrols which of the following?
    a. The strip mall along Indian School Road on Wednesdays from 4:00 p.m. to 10:00 p.m.
    b. The strip mall along Indian School Road on Fridays from 7:00 p.m. to 1:00 a.m.
    c. The neighborhoods between Roosevelt and Van Buren on Monday from 9:00 a.m. to 3:00 p.m.
    d. Between 19th Avenue and 45th Avenue from 4:00 p.m. to 10:00 p.m.

4. Officer Tiffany is reading the crime reports in her patrol area.

> All drug deals reported occur between 19th Avenue and 45th Avenue, all house break-ins occur in the neighborhoods between Roosevelt and Van Buren, and all vehicle break-ins occur by the strip mall along Indian School Road.

> Most drug deals happen on Fridays, most house break-ins occur on Mondays, and most vehicle break-ins occur on Wednesdays.

> Most drug deals happen between 8:00 p.m. and midnight, most house break-ins occur between 10:00 a.m. and 2:00 p.m., and most vehicle break-ins occur between 5:00 p.m. and 9:00 p.m.

Officer Tiffany will have the best chance of decreasing house break-ins if she patrols which of the following?
    a. The neighborhoods between Roosevelt and Van Buren on Monday from 4:00 p.m. to 10:00 p.m.
    b. The strip mall along Indian School Road on Fridays from 7:00 p.m. to 1:00 a.m.
    c. The neighborhoods between Roosevelt and Van Buren on Monday from 9:00 a.m. to 3:00 p.m.
    d. Between 19th Avenue and 45th Avenue from 9:00 a.m. to 3:00 p.m.

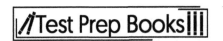

5. Officer Ryan is looking over his patrol area's crime reports.

Most stolen goods are sold between 10:00 p.m. and 2:00 a.m., most drug deals occur between 10:00 p.m. and 2:00 a.m., and most muggings occur between 9:00 p.m. and midnight.

Most illegal goods are sold on Fridays, most drug deals occur on Saturdays, and most muggings occur on Saturdays.

Illegal goods are reported to be sold between Cherry Avenue and Missouri Avenue, drug deals occur in the Conant Gardens neighborhood, and muggings occur by the dollar store off Interstate 40.

Officer Ryan will have the best chance of decreasing muggings if he patrols which of the following?
a. The Conant Gardens neighborhood on Saturdays from 9:00 p.m. to 3:00 a.m.
b. The dollar store off Interstate 40 on Saturdays from 8:00 p.m. to 1:00 a.m.
c. Between Cherry Avenue and Missouri Avenue on Saturdays from 8:00 p.m. to 1:00 a.m.
d. Between Cherry Avenue and Missouri Avenue from 9:00 p.m. to 3:00 a.m.

Use the table below to answer the following question:

Number of Cases by County in 2019			
County	Cases Filed	Cases Completed	Cases Completed Increase/Decrease From 2018
Maricopa	1512	1353	+276
Mohave	1289	1199	−105
Pima	1156	1044	−165
Pinal	1041	946	+92

6. Which county had the highest percentage of its filed cases completed in 2019?
a. Maricopa
b. Mohave
c. Pima
d. Pinal

Use the graph below to answer the question:

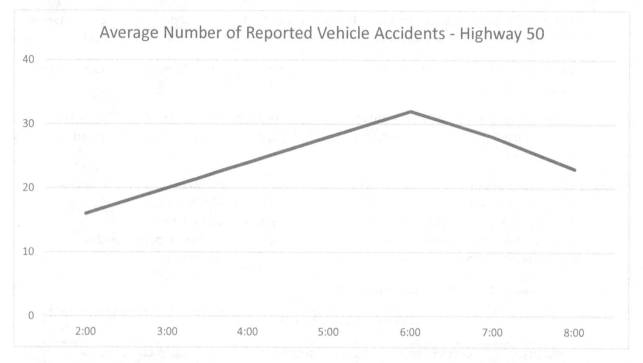

Average Number of Reported Vehicle Accidents - Highway 50

7. Which time below best represents the time that the number of vehicle accident reports start to decrease?
   a. 6:00
   b. 2:00
   c. 7:15
   d. 6:20

8. A woman is pulled over for swerving between lanes. Her papers are in order, but her speech is slurred, and she appears visibly very nervous. She was also driving 50 mph in a zone with a limit of 45 mph. Which of the following statutes would define this crime?
   a. The statute that prohibits driving while intoxicated
   b. The statute that requires all vehicles to be insured
   c. The statute that prohibits going over the designated speed limit
   d. The statute that prohibits suicide

9. Federal law has a statute that prohibits minors under twenty-one years of age from purchasing alcohol. Which of the following crimes can be defined using this statute?
   a. A man with gray hair and a long beard is found stealing beer from a convenience store.
   b. Gun shots were reportedly heard at a public park.
   c. There are reports of music being played too loud from an apartment late at night.
   d. A nightclub bouncer is reported to not be checking IDs before letting people enter the bar area.

10. OFFICER'S REPORT: I responded to a call about a missing eight-year-old child in Tempe, AZ, around midnight. When I arrived, a woman, calling herself Joan Fountain, identified herself as the mother of the lost child, James Fountain. She said the child usually never leaves the apartment complex, only going from his apartment to where his friend lives, but he has not been there and has not come back since the morning he was supposed to have left for school. He also will not answer his cell phone. She also says the school called and informed her he was absent from school that day. She seemed intoxicated and got irritated easily at my questions. Also, the child's bike was missing, and change was taken from a tray where the family kept loose coins.

Which of the following details in the report is NOT relevant to the case?
    a. The woman being intoxicated
    b. The missing bike and money
    c. The time of night
    d. The name of the mother

11. A man is discovered dead in his house, surrounded by drug paraphernalia and a half-empty bottle of liquor. Which of the following details in a case report would be the most relevant to the situation?
    a. The square footage of the house
    b. The type of shoes the man was wearing
    c. The type of drug paraphernalia found
    d. The number of officers present at the scene on arrival

12. An officer would MOST likely require backup in which of the following situations?
    a. There is a report of gang violence in a neighborhood.
    b. A young man is caught shoplifting from the grocery store.
    c. A man is accused of sexual assault at his workplace.
    d. A woman reports a missing purse containing very expensive jewelry.

13. An officer is MOST likely to ask an individual to step out of their car for inspection after pulling them over for which of the following?
    a. The driver has outdated insurance.
    b. There are five teenagers in the car with no adults present.
    c. The driver was speeding.
    d. There is a strong odor of alcohol on the driver's breath.

Reasoning

1. Which of the following is the next number in the series: 84, 80, 76, 72, 68...?
    a. 75
    b. 67
    c. 64
    d. 70

2. Which of the following is the next number in the series: 17, 18, 20, 23, 27...?
    a. 29
    b. 33
    c. 23
    d. 32

3. After school, Andrew, Matt and Geeta spend time watching television. Andrew watches more television than Geeta, but less than Matt. Which of the following lists from most to least the friends in order of how much television they watch after school?
    a. Andrew, Matt, Geeta
    b. Not enough information
    c. Geeta, Andrew, Matt
    d. Matt, Andrew, Geeta

4. Three of the following words are similar, while one is different. Which one is different?
    a. Notebook
    b. Pencil
    c. Pen
    d. Crayon

5. Which of the following is the next number in the series: 41, 30, 42, 29, 43, 28...?
    a. 30
    b. 44
    c. 43
    d. 41

6. Alejandro, Jennifer and Walt are competing in their track team's 500-meter dash. Jennifer finished behind Walt but ahead of Alejandro. Who won the race?
    a. Alejandro
    b. Jennifer
    c. Walt
    d. Not enough information

7. Which of the following is the next number in the series: 144, 133, 130, 119, 116...?
    a. 113
    b. 105
    c. 127
    d. 98

8. Three of the following words are similar, while one is different. Which one is different?
    a. Lake
    b. Ocean
    c. River
    d. Boat

9. Which of the following is the next number in the series: 288, 144, 72, 36, 18...?
    a. 4
    b. 12
    c. 6
    d. 9

10. On their driving test, Anna earned 97 points, 12 points more than Michael. Michael scored 10 points higher than Tom, who scored 6 points lower than Jaime. What was Tom's score?

    a. 109

    b. 22

    c. 75

    d. 91

11. Which of the following is the next number in the series: 3, 9, 27, 81, 243...?

    a. 486

    b. 729

    c. 121

    d. 356

Spatial Orientation, Visualization, and Memorization

Directions for Questions 1-5:

Examine the image below for two minutes then remove it from view. Answer the questions that follow the image without referring back to the image. Do not read the questions during the image review period.

1. How many people are in the room on the right?
    a. 1
    b. 2
    c. 3
    d. 4

2. How many cameras are there?
    a. 4
    b. 3
    c. 2
    d. 1

3. Which of the following items is in the room at the top?
    a. Stool
    b. Clock
    c. Camera
    d. Flag

4. What time is it on the clock?
    a. 11:15
    b. 1:55
    c. 10:30
    d. 2:35

5. How many officers are checking in at the bottom check in station?
    a. 2
    b. 1
    c. 4
    d. 3

Use the map below to answer Questions 6 and 7:

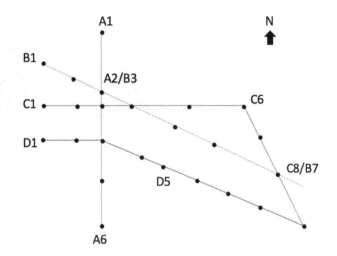

6. The map above shows the routes of subway lines in the city. Each color represents a different subway route, and each route is also labeled with a letter. Each stop in the route is identified by a black dot and a number that starts at either the western-most or northern-most stop, increasing by one at each following stop.

If Mr. Smith wants to commute from stop A2 to C9, which route would be the quickest (go through the least number of stops)?
   a. A2 to C4 to B7 to C9
   b. A2 to C4 to C6 to C9
   c. A2 to C3 to C6 to C9
   d. A2 to D3 to C9

7. The map above shows the routes of subway lines in the city. Each color represents a different subway route, and each route is also labeled with a letter. Each stop in the route is identified by a black dot and a number that starts at either the western-most or northern-most stop, increasing by one at each following stop.

Mr. Smith needs to get from stop A6 to B7, but the C line is closed off for the day. Which route would be the LEAST efficient to take (go through the greatest number of stops) but still get Mr. Smith to his destination?
   a. A6 to D3 to D8 to B7
   b. A6 to A2 to B7
   c. A6 to C3 to C6 to B7
   d. A6 to C3 to B4 to B5 to B7

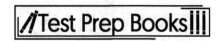

Use the map below to answer Questions 8 and 9:

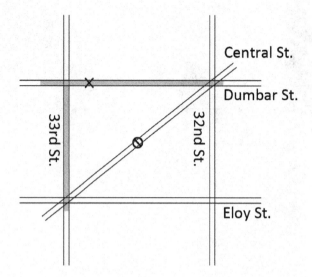

8. The map above shows the amount of traffic in a given area. The double lines indicate roads and the ones shaded grey indicate roads with heavier traffic. A crash is indicated by the symbol ✗. Closed roads are indicated with a ⊘.

According to the traffic depiction, if you were at the corner of Eloy St. and 32nd St., which route would be the fastest way to the crash site?
   a. 32nd Street to Dumbar Street
   b. 35th Street to Dumbar Street
   c. Eloy Street to 33rd Street
   d. Eloy Street to 31st Street to Dumbar Street

9. The map above shows the amount of traffic in a given area. The double lines indicate roads and the ones shaded grey indicate roads with heavier traffic. A crash is indicated by the symbol ✗. Closed roads are indicated with a ⊘.

If the black dot on the graph above represents the officer's current location, which route would have the least amount of traffic to take to the grey dot?
   a. Dumbar Street to 33rd Street to destination
   b. 32nd Street to Eloy Street to destination
   c. Central Street to destination
   d. Dumbar Street to 31st Street to Eloy Street to destination

10. Which of the following facial features would be the MOST recognizable when asked to match a face with a sketch?
   a. Medium-length hair
   b. A smiling face
   c. A cigarette in the mouth
   d. A birthmark below the eye

11. A sketch shows a man wearing sunglasses with short hair, a mustache, earrings, and a tattoo of a small cross between his eyebrows. Which part of the sketch would have to correspond most accurately with a real face to be a confirmed match?

  a. The sunglasses
  b. The short hair
  c. The earrings
  d. The tattoo of a cross

12. Which of the following details of a wanted poster would be the MOST useful information to recall when looking for a suspect?

  a. The text on the back of the poster
  b. Whether the poster is digital or printed
  c. The age of the suspect
  d. What the person is wearing in the photo

13. Where would an officer most likely find the details of the crimes committed by a suspect on a wanted poster?

  a. On the back of the poster
  b. Under the picture of the suspect in a text description
  c. By following a link on the poster
  d. By looking up the suspect's listed ID number

Information Management, Problem Sensitivity, and Situational Judgement

1. Which of the following details taken from a report would be considered the MOST meaningful?

  a. Page Park was vandalized at 10 p.m. on January 13th.
  b. The temperature was 55 degrees Fahrenheit.
  c. There were twenty-five cars at the park.
  d. There are no details on the suspect.

2. Which of the following details taken from a report would be considered the LEAST meaningful?

  a. A car was stolen in the Walmart parking lot on June 3rd.
  b. The suspect was described as most likely being poor.
  c. The suspect was said to have walked with a limp.
  d. The car license plate was 9G365.

3. OFFICER NOTES: I responded to a call at 1278 N. Laurel Drive in Phoenix, AZ, on January 3rd. When I arrived, no one answered the door after continued knocks. I looked through an open window near the door and saw a body lying motionless on the living room floor. I decided to break in the door and found a woman in her fifties who was unconscious.

Which detail from the scenario above would be filled in under an "Actions Taken" section of the police department form?

  a. The officer broke through the door.
  b. The house was at 1278 N. Laurel Drive in Phoenix, AZ, on January 3rd.
  c. The woman was unconscious upon being found.
  d. The officer acted correctly based on what he saw.

4. Police policy states that every officer needs to wear a body cam while on patrol. Which of the following scenarios might be an example of why this policy is in place?
   a. A police car is involved in an accident.
   b. A police officer uses excess force on an individual.
   c. The police officer needs to show his superiority when he is writing a report.
   d. The officer wants to have a video meeting.

5. A woman who is pulled over for speeding is found with drug paraphernalia in her vehicle. Which police policy applies to this scenario?
   a. The policy that requires a criminal's rights to be read to her when being arrested
   b. The policy that requires reasonable cause to search an individual
   c. The policy that requires officers to work during their break
   d. The policy that requires a driver's license and registration be checked upon pulling over a vehicle

Use the following witness reports for questions 6 and 7.

WITNESS REPORT 1: An elderly man I have never seen before came into the office just before noon and asked to speak privately with the boss and then, without waiting, just barged through the boss's door. About ten minutes later, I heard two gunshots, one right after the other, I think, or maybe a few minutes apart. When I went back into the office, both men were lying dead, and the gun was on the floor between them. Before the man entered the office, I asked my boss if he could come in first, of course, and he said sure. I didn't see him go in, though, but I was pretty busy, so I don't know.

WITNESS REPORT 2: Raul, a middle-aged man who worked with us at the factory and who I spoke with in the mornings occasionally before work, told me that day he was going to see the boss about wages. He didn't sound upset, but you never know with Raul. He was a mysterious fellow. I don't know when he went to the office because I didn't see him go, but I remember hearing the shots around noon because I was just about to go to lunch.

WITNESS REPORT 3: We were all about to go to lunch at noon when Raul, my partner on the factory line who comes to lunch with us every day, says he is skipping the day because he needs to speak with the boss. He had been there awhile, but he was only forty or so, not like us old timers who got on because of a whole government layoff thing. Sure, we were kind of upset about stuff here and there, but I don't think I heard him say anything really. He wouldn't talk to anyone but me about it too because it wasn't that serious and he was a private man. I mean I liked my boss. Sometimes he was mean or didn't treat us right, but he was just a man, I guess. I don't really talk about the company. I just do my work, and I don't talk to Raul really either.

WITNESS REPORT 4: I didn't really see it happen, but I knew it would. I never trust anyone in this company. They all just got hired because of some dirty government business. I didn't know or speak to Raul, or any of them, except I guess one morning we all kind of had a discussion, but I wasn't really involved, I swear! Don't question me anymore!

6. Which of the following details is most likely true?
   a. The shooting happened around noon.
   b. There was no discussion among workers that day.
   c. Raul is a very old man.
   d. Raul is shy.

7. Which witness is most likely telling the truth?
   a. Witness 1
   b. Witness 2
   c. Witness 3
   d. Witness 4

Answer Explanations

Spelling

1. C

2. C

3. B

4. D

5. D

6. D

7. D

8. B

9. B

10. C

11. B

12. D

13. C

14. A

15. D

Enforcement Vocabulary

1. C: *Partner*: a person who takes part in a plan with another person

Accomplice: a person who joins another person in the act of carrying out a plan (most likely an illegal or unethical one)

2. A: *Claim*: a declaration that something is the truth without the accompaniment of evidence

Allegation: a claim or assertion of some wrongdoing, typically made without proof

3. B: *Proceeding*: the steps of carrying out the law within an institution

Arraignment: the courtroom proceeding where a defendant is apprised of the charges against them and enters a plea of guilty or not guilty

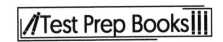

4. B: *Assault*: to attack suddenly and unlawfully

Battery: an assault where the assailant makes physical contact with another person

5. D: *Pressure*: to influence someone to do a particular thing

Coerce: to persuade an unwilling person to do something by using pressure, intimidation, or threats

6. B: *Stealing*: the act of taking a thing from somebody that isn't one's own

Embezzling: to defraud someone or to steal property (often money) entrusted into one's care

7. A: *Cleared*: to be absolved of misunderstanding or doubt

Exonerated: to be pronounced not guilty of criminal charges

8. C: *Death*: the event of a person's life ending

Fatality: a death that occurs as the result of an accident, disaster, war, or disease

9. D: *Fake*: an imitation of reality; a simulation

Forgery: to create or imitate something (e.g., an object or document) with the intent to deceive others or profit from the sale of it

10. A: *Hidden*: something kept out of sight or concealed

Latent: a thing that's hidden, or something that exists but hasn't been developed yet

11. B: *Postponement*: to hold off on a scheduled activity until a later date

Moratorium: a legal postponement or waiting period set by some authority to suspend activity

12. C: *Criminal*: someone who is guilty of a crime

Perpetrator: the person who commits a crime

13. C: *Lie*: to state a contradiction of the truth; to deceive

Prevaricate: to deliberately evade the truth or lie in order to mislead

14. A: *Guidelines*: a set of standards created for a future action

Protocol: official guidelines or procedures that must be followed

15. D: *Calm*: to make tranquil or serene

Quell: to calm, quiet, or put an end to something

Reading Comprehension

1. D: The passage directly states that the larger sensor is the main difference between the two cameras. Choices *A* and *B* may be true, but these answers do not identify the major difference between the two cameras. Choice *C* states the opposite of what the paragraph suggests is the best option for amateur photographers, so it is incorrect.

2. D: An actuary assesses risks and sets insurance premiums. While an actuary does work in insurance, the passage does not suggest that actuaries have any affiliation with hospitalists or working in a hospital, so all other choices are incorrect.

3. A: The passage focuses mainly on the problems of hard water. Choice *B* is incorrect because calcium is not good for pipes and hard surfaces. The passage does not say anything about whether water softeners are easy to install, so Choice *C* is incorrect. Choice *D* is also incorrect because the passage does offer other solutions besides vinegar.

4. C: The main point of this paragraph is that parents need to change their poor behavior at their kids' sporting events. Choice *A* is incorrect because the coaches' behavior is not mentioned in the paragraph. Choice *B* suggests that sports are bad for kids, when the paragraph is about parents' behavior, so it is incorrect. While Choice *D* may be true, it offers a specific solution to the problem, which the paragraph does not discuss.

5. B: The main point of this passage is to show how a tornado forms. Choice *A* is off base because while the passage does mention that tornadoes are dangerous, it is not the main focus of the passage. While thunderstorms are mentioned, they are not compared to tornadoes, so Choice *C* is incorrect. Choice *D* is incorrect because the passage does not discuss what to do in the event of a tornado.

6. C: The purpose of this passage is to explain how the digestive system works. Choice *A* focuses only on the liver, which is a small part of the process and not the focus of the paragraph. Choice *B* is off-track because the passage does not mention healthy foods. Choice *D* only focuses on one part of the digestive system.

7. D: The main point of this passage is to define osteoporosis. Choice *A* is incorrect because the passage does not list ways that people contract osteoporosis. Choice *B* is incorrect because the passage does not mention any treatment options. While the passage does briefly mention prevention, it does not explain how, so Choice *C* is incorrect.

8. D: The passage compares Disney cruises with Disney parks. It does not discuss how to book a cruise, so Choice *A* is incorrect. Choice *B* is incorrect because though the passage does mention some of the park attractions, it is not the main point. The passage does not mention the cost of either option, so Choice *C* is incorrect.

9. B: The point of this passage is to show what drowning looks like. Choice *A* is incorrect because while drowning is a danger of swimming, the passage doesn't include any other dangers. The passage is not intended for lifeguards specifically, but for a general audience, so Choice *C* is incorrect. There are a few signs of drowning, but the passage does not compare them; thus, *D* is incorrect.

10. C: Choice *A* is incorrect because it describes facts: Leif Erikson was the son of Erik the Red and historians debate Leif's date of birth. These are not opinions. Choice *B* is incorrect; that Erikson called the land Vinland is a verifiable fact as is Choice *D* because he did contact the natives almost 500 years

before Columbus. Choice *C* is the correct answer because it is the author's opinion that Erikson deserves more credit. That, in fact, is his conclusion in the piece, but another person could argue that Columbus or another explorer deserves more credit for opening up the New World to exploration. Rather than being an incontrovertible fact, it is a subjective value claim.

11. B: Choice *B* is correct because it accurately identifies the author's statement that Erikson deserves more credit than he has received for being the first European to explore the New World. Choice *A* is incorrect because the author aims to go beyond describing Erikson as a mere legendary Viking. Choice *C* is incorrect because the author does not focus on Erikson's motivations, let alone name the spreading of Christianity as his primary objective. Choice *D* is incorrect because it is a premise that Erikson contacted the natives 500 years before Columbus, which is simply a part of supporting the author's conclusion.

12. D: Choice *A* is incorrect because the author never addresses the Vikings' state of mind or emotions. Choice *B* is incorrect because the author does not elaborate on Erikson's exile and whether he would have become an explorer if not for his banishment. Choice *C* is incorrect because there is not enough information to support this premise. It is unclear whether Erikson informed the King of Norway of his finding. Although it is true that the King did not send a follow-up expedition, he could have simply chosen not to expend the resources after receiving Erikson's news. It is not possible to logically infer whether Erikson told him. Choice *D* is correct because there are two examples—Leif Erikson's date of birth and what happened during the encounter with the natives—of historians having trouble pinning down important dates in Viking history.

13. B: But in fact, there is not much substance to such speculation, and most anti-Stratfordian arguments can be refuted with a little background about Shakespeare's time and upbringing. The thesis is a statement that contains the author's topic and main idea. The main purpose of this article is to use historical evidence to provide counterarguments to anti-Stratfordians. Choice *A* is simply a definition; Choice *C* is a supporting detail, not a main idea; and Choice *D* represents an idea of anti-Stratfordians, not the author's opinion.

14. C: It is an example of a rhetorical question. This requires readers to be familiar with different types of rhetorical devices. A rhetorical question is a question that is asked not to obtain an answer but to encourage readers to more deeply consider an issue.

15. B: By explaining grade school curriculum in Shakespeare's time. This question asks readers to refer to the organizational structure of the article and demonstrate understanding of how the author provides details to support their argument. This particular detail can be found in the second paragraph: "even though he did not attend university, grade school education in Shakespeare's time was actually quite rigorous."

16. A: It most closely means busy. This is a vocabulary question that can be answered using context clues. Other sentences in the paragraph describe London as "the most populous city in England" filled with "crowds of people," giving an image of a busy city full of people. Choice *B* is incorrect because London was in Shakespeare's home country, not a foreign one. Choice *C* is not mentioned in the passage. Choice *D* is not a good answer choice because the passage describes how London was a popular and important city, probably not an undeveloped one.

17. B: Choice *B* is correct because the author is trying to demonstrate the main idea, which is that heat loss is proportional to surface area, and so they compare two animals with different surface areas to clarify the main point. Choice *A* is incorrect because the author uses elephants and anteaters to prove a point, that heat loss is proportional to surface area, not to express an opinion. Choice *C* is incorrect because though the author does use them to show differences, they do so in order to give examples that prove the above points, so Choice *C* is not the best answer. Choice *D* is incorrect because there is no language to indicate favoritism between the two animals.

18. C: Because of the way that the author addresses the reader, and also the colloquial language that the author uses (i.e., "let me explain," "so," "well," didn't," "you would look silly," etc.), *C* is the best answer because it has a much more casual tone than the usual informative article. Choice *A* may be a tempting choice because the author says the "fact" that most of one's heat is lost through their head is a "lie," and that someone who does not wear a shirt in the cold looks silly, but it only happens twice within all the diction of the passage and it does not give an overall tone of harshness. *B* is incorrect because again, while not necessarily nice, the language does not carry an angry charge. The author is clearly not indifferent to the subject because of the passionate language that they use, so *D* is incorrect.

19. A: The author gives logical examples and reasons in order to prove that most of one's heat is not lost through their head, therefore *A* is correct. *B* is incorrect because there is not much emotionally charged language in this selection, and even the small amount present is greatly outnumbered by the facts and evidence. *C* is incorrect because there is no mention of ethics or morals in this selection. *D* is incorrect because the author never qualifies himself as someone who has the authority to be writing on this topic.

20. C: Choice *C* is correct because Joseph Bruin bought hundreds of slaves during the years 1844 to 1861. Choice *A* is incorrect because the seaport is noted as "thriving"; also, the slave trading companies were noted as being "lucrative." Choice *B* is incorrect because the slave traders actually built both office structures and slave holding buildings in downtown Alexandria; there is no mention of renting, or of landlords.

21. A: Choice *A* contains information provided in the passage; therefore, the statement is true. Choice *B* is false because the passage infers that Joseph Bruin was notorious as a slave trader; in fact, two sisters tried to run away from Joseph Bruin. Choice *C* is false because the slave pen was not four stories high; the passage specifically noted that the slave pen was two stories high. Choice *D* is false because the passage does not refer to Union or Confederate soldiers, and the Bruin Slave Jail was what became the Fairfax County courthouse.

22. C: The purpose of the passage is to shed light on the history of Joseph Bruin's Slave Jail and what became of it. Choice *A* is incorrect because while the two sisters are mentioned in the story to provide details, they are not the main purpose of the story. Choice *B* is incorrect because while the beginning of the story contains the information about the town and its slave business, this answer option leaves out the fact that the passage is focused on one slave jail in particular and omits anything about the conclusion of the passage, which is actually key in the main focus of the passage—how Joseph Bruin's Slave Jail came about and what became of it. Choice *D* is incorrect because the point of the passage is not about where the historical Bruin Slave Jail currently stands, but the history behind it.

23. C: Choice *C* is true as noted in the second sentence of the passage: Emotional Intelligence (EI) includes developing the ability to know one's own emotions, to regulate impulses and emotions, and to use interpersonal communication skills with ease while dealing with other people. It makes sense that someone with well-developed emotional intelligence will have a good handle on understanding his or her emotions and be able to regulate impulses and emotions and use honed interpersonal communication skills. Because the details in Choice *A* and Choice *B* are examples of how an emotionally intelligent leader operates, they are not the best choice for the definition of the term *emotional*

intelligence. They are qualities observed in an EI leader. Choice *D* is not a definition of EI so Choice *D* is incorrect.

24. D: The qualities of an unsuccessful leader possessing a transactional leadership style are listed in the passage. Choices *A* and *B* are incorrect because these options reflect the qualities of a successful leader. Choice *C*'s options are definitely not characteristics of a successful leader; however, they are not presented in the passage and readers should do their best to ignore such options.

25. D: Even though some choices may be true of successful leaders, the best answer must be supported by subpoints in the passage. Therefore, Choices *A* and *C* are incorrect. Choice *B* is incorrect because uncompromising transactional leadership styles squelch success.

26. B: Readers should carefully focus their attention on the beginning of the passage to answer this series of questions. Even though the sentences may be worded a bit differently, all but one statement is true. It presents a false idea that descriptive details are not necessary until the climax of the story. Even if one does not read the passage, he or she probably knows that all good writing begins with descriptive details to develop the main theme the writer intends for the narrative.

27. B: Choice *B* is correct because of the opening statement that reads, "Learning how to write a ten-minute play may seem like a monumental task at first; but, if you follow a simple creative writing strategy, similar to writing a narrative story, you will be able to write a successful drama." To suggest that a ten-minute play is accessible does not imply any timeline, nor does the passage mention how long a playwright spends with revisions and rewrites. So, Choice *A* is incorrect. None of the remaining choices are supported by points in the passage.

28. C: This choice allows room for the fact that not all people who attempt to write a play will find it easy. If the writer follows the basic principles of narrative writing described in the passage, however, writing a play does not have to be an excruciating experience. None of the other options can be supported by points from the passage.

29. A: The passage discusses recent technological advances in cars and suggests that this trend will continue in the future with self-driving cars. Choice *B* and *C* are not true, so these are both incorrect. Choice *D* is also incorrect because the passage suggests continuing growth in technology, not a peak.

30. B: The information in the second sentence further explains the draft process and thus supports the first sentence. It does not contradict the first sentence, so *A* is incorrect. Choices *C* and *D* are incorrect because the second sentence does not restate or offer a solution to the first.

31. B: The first sentence identifies Facebook as the most popular social media site with 1 billion users. The second sentence states that Instagram only has 100 million users, but is the most used. This contradicts the original sentence, so all other answers are incorrect.

32. A: The first sentence states that there are eight phases to the moon cycle. The second sentence discusses first quarter, which is one of the phases of the moon. Therefore, the second sentence provides an example of the first sentence.

33. C: The first sentence discusses the effects of the terror attacks of September 11, 2001. The second sentence states that the Department of Homeland Security was created in response to the terror attacks, so it states an effect of the first sentence.

34. A: The first sentence describes the life cycle of annuals. The second sentence describes the life cycle of perennials, making a contrast between the way annuals grow and the way perennials grow.

35. D: The first sentence describes how viruses can affect a PC. The second sentence offers a solution to the problem of viruses and malware on a PC.

36. C: The first sentence describes cage-free chickens as not being confined to a cage, suggesting they are treated humanely. The second sentence disputes the first sentence, showing that cage-free chickens are inhumanely confined to a larger area with many other chickens, never seeing the outdoors.

37. B: The first sentence states that schools are no longer teaching cursive handwriting. The second sentence shows that as an effect of the first sentence, students will no longer be able to read or write cursive handwriting.

38. B: The first sentence states that air travel has changed in the last decade. The second sentence provides examples of the changes that have occurred.

39. A: The first sentence discusses how fragrances and other chemicals in products can cause skin reactions. The second sentence states that many products contain ingredients that cause skin allergies, restating the same information from the first sentence.

Mathematics

1. B: Instead of multiplying these out, the product can be estimated by using $18 \times 10 = 180$. The error here should be lower than 15, since it is rounded to the nearest integer, and the numbers add to something less than 30.

2. C: 85% of a number means multiplying that number by 0.85. So, $0.85 \times 20 = \frac{85}{100} \times \frac{20}{1}$, which can be simplified to:

$$\frac{17}{20} \times \frac{20}{1} = 17$$

3. A: To find the fraction of the bill that the first three people pay, the fractions need to be added, which means finding common denominator. The common denominator will be 60.

$$\frac{1}{5} + \frac{1}{4} + \frac{1}{3} = \frac{12}{60} + \frac{15}{60} + \frac{20}{60} = \frac{47}{60}$$

The remainder of the bill is:

$$1 - \frac{47}{60} = \frac{60}{60} - \frac{47}{60} = \frac{13}{60}$$

4. B: 30% is 3/10. The number itself must be 10/3 of 6, or:

$$\frac{10}{3} \times 6 = 10 \times 2 = 20$$

5. A: These numbers to improper fractions: $\frac{11}{3} - \frac{9}{5}$. Take 15 as a common denominator:

$$\frac{11}{3} - \frac{9}{5} =: \frac{55}{15} - \frac{27}{15} = \frac{28}{15} = 1\frac{13}{15} \text{ (when rewritten to get rid of the partial fraction)}$$

6. A: Dividing by 98 can be approximated by dividing by 100, which would mean shifting the decimal point of the numerator to the left by 2. The result is 4.2 and rounds to 4.

7. B: $4\frac{1}{3} + 3\frac{3}{4} = 4 + 3 + \frac{1}{3} + \frac{3}{4} = 7 + \frac{1}{3} + \frac{3}{4}$. Adding the fractions gives:

$$\frac{1}{3} + \frac{3}{4} = \frac{4}{12} + \frac{9}{12} = \frac{13}{12} = 1 + \frac{1}{12}$$

Thus:

$$7 + \frac{1}{3} + \frac{3}{4} = 7 + 1 + \frac{1}{12} = 8\frac{1}{12}$$

8. C: The average is calculated by adding all six numbers, then dividing by 6. The first five numbers have a sum of 25. If the total divided by 6 is equal to 6, then the total itself must be 36. The sixth number must be 36 − 25 = 11.

9. B: Multiplying by 10^{-3} means moving the decimal point three places to the left, putting in zeroes as necessary.

10. B: $\frac{5}{2} \div \frac{1}{3} = \frac{5}{2} \times \frac{3}{1} = \frac{15}{2} = 7.5$.

11. A: The total fraction taken up by green and red shirts will be:

$$\frac{1}{3} + \frac{2}{5} = \frac{5}{15} + \frac{6}{15} = \frac{11}{15}$$

The remaining fraction is:

$$1 - \frac{11}{15} = \frac{15}{15} - \frac{11}{15} = \frac{4}{15}$$

12. C: If she has used 1/3 of the paint, she has 2/3 remaining. $2\frac{1}{2}$ gallons are the same as $\frac{5}{2}$ gallons. The calculation is:

$$\frac{2}{3} \times \frac{5}{2} = \frac{5}{3} = 1\frac{2}{3} \text{ gallons}$$

13. B: The dress costs $15. Then you need to find 8% of $15, by multiplying 15 times .08. This gives you $1.20. Add that to $15 to get $16.20.

14. D: Start by substituting .5 into the equation so that you have $2(.5) + \frac{10}{.5}$. You can then solve this to get $1 + 20 = 21$.

15. B: The hundredths place is the second place after the decimal. In this case it is the 5. The number following it is a 6, so you would round up to get 23.16.

Grammar

1. B: Stacked modifying nouns such as this example are untangled by starting from the end and adding words as necessary to provide meaning. In this case, a *guide* to *improving relations* between *managers* and *employees*. Choice B is correct, as it unstacks the nouns in the correct order and also makes logical sense. Choices C and D do not define the item first as a guide. Choice A does identify as a guide but confuses the order of the remaining descriptors.

2. C: The second sentence tells of an unexpected outcome of the first sentence. Choice A, Choice B, and Choice D indicate a logical progression, which does not match this surprise. Only Choice C indicates this unexpected twist.

3. B: Choice A, Choice C, and Choice D all relate facts but do not present the kind of general statement that would serve as an effective summary or conclusion. Choice B is correct.

4. B: Answer Choice A uses the plural form of the verb, when the subject is the pronoun *none*, which needs a singular verb. C also uses the wrong verb form and uses the word *all* in place of *none*, which doesn't make sense in the context of the sentence. D uses *all* again, and is missing the comma, which is necessary to set the dependent clause off from the independent clause.

5. C: In this answer, the article and subject agree, and the subject and predicate agree. Answer Choice A is incorrect because the article *an* and *issues* do not agree in number. B is incorrect because an article is needed before *important issue*. D is incorrect because the plural subject *issues* does not agree with the singular verb *is*.

6. D: Choices A and C use additional words and phrases that aren't necessary. B is more concise but uses the present tense of *is*. This does not agree with the rest of the sentence, which uses past tense. The best choice is D, which uses the most concise sentence structure and is grammatically correct.

7. C: Choice A is missing the word *that*, which is necessary for the sentence to make sense. Choice B pluralizes *trains* and uses the singular form of the word *include*, so it does not agree with the word *set*. Choice D changes the verb to *were*, which is in plural form and does not agree with the singular subject.

8. A: Choices B and D both use the expression *attributed to the fact* incorrectly. It can only be attributed *to* the fact, not *with* or *in* the fact. Choice C incorrectly uses a gerund, *saying,* when it should use the present tense of the verb *say*.

9. B: Choice B is correct because it uses correct parallel structure of plural nouns. Choice A is incorrect because the word *accessory* is in singular form. Choice C is incorrect because it pluralizes *makeup*, which is already in plural form. Choice D is incorrect because it again uses the singular *accessory*, and it uses the singular *shoe*.

10. D: In a cause/effect relationship, it is correct to use the word because in the clausal part of the sentence. This can eliminate both Choices A and C which don't clearly show the cause/effect relationship. Choice B is incorrect because it uses the present tense, when the first part of the sentence is in the past tense. It makes grammatical sense for both parts of the sentence to be in present tense.

11. A: In answer Choice B, the present tense form of the verb *consider* creates an independent clause joined to another independent clause with only a comma, which is a comma splice and grammatically

incorrect. Choices *C* and *D* use the possessive form of *its*, when it should be the contraction *it's* for *it is*. Choice *D* also includes incorrect comma placement.

12. C: The original sentence states that firefighting is dangerous, making it necessary for firefighters to wear protective gear. The portion of the sentence that needs to be rewritten focuses on the gear, not the dangers of firefighting. *A, B,* and *D* all discuss the danger, not the gear, so *C* is the correct answer.

13. D: The original sentence states that though the sites are popular, they can be dangerous for teens, so *D* is the best choice. Choice *A* does state that there is danger, but it doesn't identify teens and limits it to just one site. Choice *B* repeats the statement from the beginning of the sentence, and *C* says the sites are used too much, which is not the point made in the original sentence.

14. B: The original sentence focuses on how politicians are using the student debt issue to their advantage, so *B* is the best answer choice. Choice *A* says politicians want students' votes, but suggests that it is the reason for student loan debt, which is incorrect. Choice *C* shifts the focus to voters, when the sentence is really about politicians. Choice *D* is vague and doesn't best restate the original meaning of the sentence.

15. A: This answer best matches the meaning of the original sentence, which states that seasoned runners offer advice to new runners because they have complaints of injuries. Choice *B* may be true, but it doesn't mention the complaints of injuries by new runners. Choice *C* may also be true, but it does not match the original meaning of the sentence. Choice *D* does not make sense in the context of the sentence.

Verbal Expression

1. C: The man's jacket missing is the only incident where a person's personal property was taken. Choices *A, B,* and *D* do not match this definition of theft.

2. A: A man exposing himself in public is the only situation that matches the definition of public indecency. Choices *B, C,* and *D* have definitions that relate to different crimes.

3. A: The question specifically asks for when vehicle break-ins occur; therefore, to determine the correct choice, the data that relates specifically to vehicle break-ins should be examined. From the given information, most vehicle break-ins happen at the strip mall along Indian School Road on Wednesdays from 5:00 p.m. to 9:00 p.m., so the best time to prevent these break-ins would be to arrive at the location an hour early and stay an hour later to catch all potential break-ins.

4. C: This question is regarding only house break-ins, which, according to the data given, occur between Roosevelt and Van Buren on Mondays from 10:00 a.m. to 2:00 p.m. The remaining choices, although the time or day may be correct, do not list the correct area according to the report.

5. B: This question is regarding only muggings, which, according to the data given, occur by the dollar store off Interstate 40 on Saturdays between 9:00 p.m. and midnight. The remaining choices, although the time or day may be correct, do not list the correct area according to the report.

6. B: The needed information can be found by looking at each title on the chart. Only the county, the number of cases filed, and the cases completed are relevant to the question, meaning the Cases Completed Increase/Decrease From 2018 information is not needed. Then, by dividing the number of completed cases by the number of cases filed for each county, the percentage of completed cases can be found, proving that although Maricopa had the most cases, Mohave had the highest completion percentage (93 percent).

7. D: By following the labels on the graph, the time can be found by looking at the numbers at the bottom of the image. The numbers on the side of the graph represent the amount, increasing as they go upward. By identifying the point on the graph where the slope starts to decrease, the answer can be traced back to the time at the bottom. However, the highest point on the graph point lies right on the 6:00 p.m. time slot, meaning that the approximate time is between 6:00 and 6:30.

8. A: The crime that could possibly relate the most to this case, based on the driver's slurred speech and irresponsible driving, would be that she is intoxicated. It is described that her papers are in order, implying her insurance was up to date, making Choice *B* incorrect. Choice *C* is incorrect because even though the state law had regulated the speed limit in the area to 45 mph, the driver could not be considered to be speeding if she was only driving 5 mph over the limit. Choice *D* is also incorrect because there is no indication the driver is suicidal.

9. D: Although not explicitly stated in the scenario, the logical outcome will most likely result in the underage drinking of minors as defined by the statute. The remaining choices, although possible crimes in their own respect, still do not match the statute given because they cannot be related to the incident in a logical way.

10. A: Even though the mother's state of mind may be questionable, it does not relate to the case of the missing child and will do little to help solve the problem. Choice *B,* the information about the lost bike and money may lead to where the child may have gone, and Choice *C,* the time of night, and Choice *D,* the name of the mother, are important details to frame the background of the story.

11. C: Discovering what type of paraphernalia was possibly used could lead to a cause of death and is the only information relevant to the man's death. The remaining choices, although detailing information related to the scene, have no direct influence on the case of how the man died and do not provide insight on how the case can be solved.

12. A: Gang violence could involve multiple, dangerous individuals, so for the officer's protection it would be best to call for backup in this instance. Choice *B*, Choice *C*, and Choice *D* all are minor, non-violent crimes involving few people; therefore, they would not necessarily require an officer to call for backup assistance.

13. D: Only if the officer has very reasonable cause to further investigate an individual should they take such action. However, if the smell of alcohol is too strong for an officer not to miss, there is a just cause in asking the individual to step out of their car because they could possibly be intoxicated and cause harm to others while behind the wheel. Choice *A*, Choice *B*, and Choice *C* do not give enough evidence that the driver is suspicious of anything other than a minor traffic violation.

Reasoning

1. C: The next number in the series is 64. In this series, each successive number is 4 less than the number that preceded it. So, to find the next number in the series, subtract 4 from the previous number.

2. D: The next number in the series is 32. In this series, the numbers increase by *one more with each successive number*. So, there is an increase of 1 between the first two numbers, an increase of 2 between the second and third numbers, an increase of 3 between the third and fourth numbers, and an

increase of 4 between the fourth and fifth numbers. The next number in the series should be 5 more than the last number given.

3. D: The correct answer is Matt, Andrew, Geeta. According to the prompt, Andrew watches more television than Geeta. Since the goal is to rank the friends in order of how much television they watch *from most to least*, the list should read the following way so far: Andrew, Geeta. The prompt goes on to say that Andrew watches less television than Matt, so Matt must be added to the list above Andrew.

4. A: The word *notebook* is not like the other three. A pencil, pen, and crayon can all be used to write or draw. A notebook is something that is written or drawn *in*, rendering it different from the other three words.

5. B: The next number in the series is 44. Beginning with the first number in the series, every other number *increases by 1*. Beginning with the second number, every other number *decreases by 1*. So, to find the next number in the series, decide which pattern the missing number should continue. The missing number should continue the pattern of increasing by 1 starting with the first number in the series. Looking only at that pattern, the series reads 41…42…43. Continuing that pattern, the missing number should be 44.

6. D: Out of this group of three, Walt came in first. However, it's unclear who else on the team is participating in this race. Thus, there is insufficient information to determine whether or not Walt won the race.

7. B: The next number in the series is 105. In this series, the numbers are decreasing. The gap between each number is either 11 or 3. Following this pattern, the next number should be 11 less than the last number.

8. D: The word *boat* is not like the other three. A lake, ocean, and river are all bodies of water. A boat is a vessel used to traverse bodies of water, rendering it different from the other three words.

9. D: The next number in the series is 9. In this series, each successive number decreases by half.

10. C: Tom's score was 75. According to the prompt, Anna earned 97 points, which was 12 more than Michael. Michael earned 85 points, which is 10 more than Tom, which would give Tom 75 points.

11. B: The next number in the series is 729. In this series, each number is multiplied by 3 to get the next number, so the next number would be 243×3, which is 729.

Spatial Orientation, Visualization, and Memorization

1. B

2. C

3. D

4. B

5. A

6. A: Route stops may have multiple names because they pass through multiple lines. Route A only passes through five stops because it travels along the straight B line even though the directions suggest that different lines are involved because of the intersections. Although Choice *D* has the simplest instructions, it will actually pass through more stops when counted.

7. A: Because the information in the question states that line C is closed, only Choices *A* and *B* can be used to reach the destination (Choices *C* and *D* both include the closed line). Choice *B* would pass through eight stops, one less than the number of stops of Choice *A*.

8. D: 32nd Street is the street that has the least amount of red (traffic) that can reach the street with the accident. Choice *A*, taking 33rd Street, would be a delay, especially at the intersection by the accident; Choice *B*, 35th Street, is not listed on the map; and Choice *C*, taking Dumbar Street all the way to the accident, could also cause delays because most of the street is depicted as being red.

9. B: Although Choice *C* would normally be the quickest route because it is a straight line to the destination, Central Street is depicted as being closed. Therefore, the next fastest route to take would be Choice *B* because there is less traffic than the other choices, and it will lead directly to the destination using the streets depicted on the map.

10. D: Uncommon features that may be unique to an individual will be the most helpful to take note of when recalling faces to match sketches and narrow down options. A birthmark on a face is easily recognizable and uncommon enough to help identify matching sketches. Choice *A*, hair length, and Choice *B*, a smiling face, can be easily changed or found on any number of people at a given time, and Choice *C*, the cigarette, could be left out of a drawing.

11. D: Sketches will not always match a face exactly, so when finding matching sketches, general information or items that can be easily removed may be slightly different in the sketch than in person. Tattoos, however, cannot be changed or removed very easily, so it is the most likely that a sketch of a man that contains a corresponding tattoo is a match.

12. C: The most important information on a wanted poster will be the information that helps an officer find and identify a suspect. Only the age of the suspect corresponds to a trait that can be visually recognizable when searching for the individual. Choice *A*, the text on the back of the poster, and Choice *B*, whether the poster is digital or printed, will most likely be unrelated to the suspect, and Choice *D*, what the person is wearing, could be hard to identify because it can be so easily changed.

13. B: Most wanted posters are formatted in a similar way to be easily recognized and read without having to look up additional information in other sources. The details of crimes committed by the suspect will usually be located under their photo in a text description.

Information Management, Problem Sensitivity, and Situational Judgement

1. A: Important details involve information that can be useful to accurately report and solve the crime. Exact details of when and where the crime occurred is the most useful when detailing the case. Choice *B*, the temperature, is unrelated to the crime, and Choice *C*, the number of cars at the park, is too large to be useful. The fact that there are no details on a suspect, Choice *D*, is unimportant because it does not help solve the case either.

2. B: The suspect being poor will not be useful in solving the case because it is too general a description of the culprit to be objectively identifiable. The remaining choices all include information that is related to the crime that can be used to describe the exact incident and identify the culprit because of their singular details.

3. A: The "Actions Taken" section can be interpreted to mean what actions the officer took related to the incident (breaking through the door). Choice *B* and Choice *D* are observed details, and Choice *D* is a judgment based on *how* the officer acted—all information that belongs on other sections of the report.

4. B: The body cam policy is in place to check the power of individual officers and ensure they are acting within the boundaries of the law as well as to record video proof of incidents as they occur. A police officer using excess force is the only scenario where a body cam would be used as proof of a possible misuse of power.

5. B: The only case where a police officer would be allowed to search a vehicle after pulling it over would be if they had probable cause that the driver was concealing something. In this case, even though the exact details of the scenario are not given, it can be logically deduced that the reason the paraphernalia was found was because the officer was able to search the vehicle with probable cause.

6. A: The fact that repeats itself most often in each of the witness's reports is that the shooting took place around the workers' lunchtime, which was noon. There is also little reason indicated as to why the witnesses would lie about the time. The remaining choices, although they may also be true, are not verified by the repeated accounts of the different witnesses.

7. B: The only witness who does not contradict some of their information or is not too emotionally involved in their details is witness 2 because they are able to give a clear, concise detailing of what they observed on the day of the crime. Their answers are given in an honest way that does not try to actively deny any events that took place in a defensive way.

Dear Police Test Taker,

We would like to start by thanking you for purchasing this study guide for your police exam. We hope that we exceeded your expectations.

Our goal in creating this study guide was to cover all of the topics that you will see on the test. We also strove to make our practice questions as similar as possible to what you will encounter on test day. With that being said, if you found something that you feel was not up to your standards, please send us an email and let us know.

We have study guides in a wide variety of fields. If you're interested in one, try searching for it on Amazon or send us an email.

Thanks Again and Happy Testing!
Product Development Team
info@studyguideteam.com

FREE Test Taking Tips DVD Offer

To help us better serve you, we have developed a Test Taking Tips DVD that we would like to give you for FREE. **This DVD covers world-class test taking tips that you can use to be even more successful when you are taking your test.**

All that we ask is that you email us your feedback about your study guide. Please let us know what you thought about it – whether that is good, bad or indifferent.

To get your **FREE Test Taking Tips DVD**, email freedvd@studyguideteam.com with "FREE DVD" in the subject line and the following information in the body of the email:

     a. The title of your study guide.

     b. Your product rating on a scale of 1-5, with 5 being the highest rating.

     c. Your feedback about the study guide. What did you think of it?

     d. Your full name and shipping address to send your free DVD.

If you have any questions or concerns, please don't hesitate to contact us at freedvd@studyguideteam.com.

Thanks again!

CPSIA information can be obtained
at www.ICGtesting.com
Printed in the USA
BVHW051021131021
618824BV00009B/105